'Christ gave some to be prophets...' Proph
who have the extraordinary courage to spea
to hear it. Sue Parfitt's courage, not only t
and ecological crises we face, but literall
highlight it—whatever we think about the ta
respect and gratitude. Her book gives a clear and cogent account of the crisis we are in and of her response to the question 'What would Jesus do?'

**Olivia Graham — Bishop of Reading**

In this captivating book—steeped in the wisdom of scripture, realism, practical guidance and adorned with personal narratives—Sue Parfitt's words resonate with prophetic fervor. Demonstrating that you never retire from the Kingdom, Sue calls upon us to heed the urgent call of Jesus and live lives which embody justice, love and compassion. Read this book. Weep. Pray and act. The Kingdom is calling.

**Rev'd Jon Swales MBE — Priest, Theologian and Climate Activist**

For Christians, and all those whose lives are enriched by a deep spirituality, Sue Parfitt's *Bodies on the Line* provides a compelling read. As she so eloquently demonstrates, there is a spirit in all of us that demands an urgent, compassionate and non-violent response to the climate crisis which now engulfs us. A failure to respond is a breach of trust with our own humanity and with the whole of humankind.

**Jonathon Porritt — Author, *Capitalism As If the World Matters***

What does it mean today to follow the hard road of Jesus and the first Christians? In this compelling personal testimony, Rev'd Sue Parfitt shows how it can mean putting our bodies on the line—risking arrest and imprisonment in protest against today's principalities and powers as they threaten the destruction of our planet home.

**Peter Armstrong — Filmmaker; Author, *Not for Nothing: Searching for a Meaningful Life***

This is a marvelous small book--a true guide for Christians, and anyone of good heart, as we come up against the greatest crisis our species has ever faced. Read it, and then act on it!

**Bill McKibben — Founder, 350.org and Third Act**

This is a must-read for all Christians! Sue Parfitt challenges us to the core with a depth of insight into the human condition, holy Scripture and the reality of our precarious future.

**Laurie Green — Bishop Emeritus; Author, *Blessed Are the Poor? Urban Poverty and the Church***

Creation faces an existential threat, yet worship of the Creator carries on much as it always has within our churches, without discernment of a Christian response to the crisis. Representing the fruits of her long experience as both contemplative and activist, Sue Parfitt's book is the one many of us have been waiting for, an answer to prayer.

**Martin Davis — Founder member, Green Christian**

Why does octogenarian priest, and retired psychotherapist, The Revd. Sue Parfitt sit down on the motorway in an attempt to get arrested and have a day in court? She wishes to bear witness to the truth as it is in Jesus—who confronted injustice in the name of compassion and love—and to bear witness to the injustices of increasing climate change. Other Christians may bear that witness in different ways; but this book powerfully calls on all Christians to ask what they are doing in God's name to seek to avert what is now almost inevitable disaster.

**Rt Revd Dr David J Atkinson — Former Bishop of Thetford; Author, *Renewing the Face of the Earth***

*Bodies on the Line* is more than another 'call to action' on the climate emergency. It's a powerful, well-argued, and lucidly written challenge to all Christians, drawing on the psychology of denial and emotions, insights from spirituality and family therapy and psychotherapy. Most importantly, for Christians particularly, Sue presents her understanding of Jesus as a radical, non-violent practitioner of civil disobedience in the cause of Truth.

**Prof. John Carpenter — School for Policy Studies, University of Bristol**

A timely and vital work that is a bold and brave commentary on all things climate and activism.

**Amy Dartington, Environment and Sustainability Manager, Diocese of Bristol**

This is a book for every Christian to read: those who know a lot or a little about the climate and biodiversity crises; those who know a lot or a little about civil disobedience. Clear and beautifully written, *Bodies on the Line* contains Biblical, spiritual and practical wisdom, carefully examining from a Christian perspective the imperative for protest and all aspects of civil disobedience in this time of climate and environmental breakdown.

**Deborah Tomkins – Co-Chair, Green Christian**

This important book gives a first hand insight into the motivations and intentions of some of the UK's most prolific climate activists. The chapter on non violent direct action and the Christian faith is particularly compelling, giving huge insight into why christian climate activists put their bodies on the line. You might not agree with everything that the author says, but you cannot doubt her courage, sincerity and integrity in saying it.

**Revd Canon Jonnie Parkin – Canon Missioner, Bristol Cathedral**

Revd. Sue Parfitt weaves a strong argument for why Christians and others ought to act on climate change.Whether new to activism or someone who acted on their beliefs before, all readers will find some great pearls of wisdom in this book.. This great readable book is a manual for aspiring climate change activists. It will help put our bodies more on the line towards climate justice and a more sustainable future.

**Mazin Qumsiyeh – Founder / Director, Palestine Institute for Biodiversity and Sustainability; Bethlehem University, Palestine**

This challenging book is essential reading for Christians but will also resonate deeply with non-religious climate activists seeking new insights into faith-based activism. It is a book about courage, compassion and sacrifice; a source of wisdom for anyone who believes that faith, when coupled with action, is central to meeting the challenge that confronts us.

**Prof. Colin Davis, Department of Psychology, University of Bristol**

I challenge any 'person of conscience' (as Desmond Tutu put it) to read this book without coming to a strong sense of sympathy with this elderly lady and gratitude for all she stands for.

**David W Golding – Former Associate of the Institute of Sustainability**

Sue weaves spirituality, theology, story telling and the practical into a beautiful account of what it means for a Christian to respond meaningfully to the climate crisis. This is a book for those who are wondering why Christians are taking direct action as well for those who are wondering what more they can do beyond reducing, reusing, and recycling.

**Melanie Nazareth – Barrister, climate activist**

For anyone in any doubt about whether we have a biblical mandate as Christians to use civil resistance in the face of governments' inertia in response to the climate crisis, this book will lay that to rest. Compelling, motivating and authentic, written by a determined climate protester who will not be silenced.

**Dr Ruth Valerio – Global Advocacy and Influencing Director, Tearfund**

Whether you agree with those who seek to move the government and the wider population through civil disobedience and resistance, this is the book for understanding why many Christians have adopted such actions. The severity of the climate crisis has become ever more clear by the events of 2022 and the first half of 2023. In "the era of global boiling" we need to heed voices like that of Parfitt's.

**Revd. Dr. Darrell D. Hannah – Chair of Operation Noah**

# BODIES ON THE LINE

## CHRISTIANS, CIVIL RESISTANCE AND THE CLIMATE CRISIS

SUE PARFITT

**Published by LAB / ORA Press**
St. Peter's Community Centre
Charles Street
Coventry
CV1 5NP
United Kingdom

Published in the UK in 2023

ISBN: 978-1-7397162-8-8
Ebook ISBN: 978-1-7397162-9-5

Printed and bound in the United Kingdom by IngramSpark

*This book is dedicated, with gratitude and love, to the members of Christian Climate Action and in particular to Phil Kingston, a Founder Member of Christian Climate Action and of Grandparents for a Safe Earth. Phil is an inspiration to many. He introduced me to Christian Climate Action in 2017, having pulled me through one of the darkest periods of my life, after the death of my husband Graeme.*

# AUTHOR'S NOTE

The inspiration for this book comes first of all from John Dear, who wrote the most influential text around on civil disobedience in the 1990s. *The Sacrament of Civil Disobedience* had been out of print for many years, but a new revised edition was published towards the end of 2022, edited and produced by Chris Donald and myself. Working with the Passionists—a Catholic Order committed to climate crisis resistance—Chris set up Lab/ora Press, a new publishing imprint, designed to re-publish theological works that were now out of print. He has therefore been able to offer *The Sacrament of Civil Disobedience* to a new contemporary audience.

In the Editors' note to this new edition, I tell the story of how I first came across John's original book in a little library in Hebron in Palestine, belonging to the American human rights organisation, Community Peacemaker Teams. And I explain what an impression it made upon me. But while helping revise John's text for the new edition, it became clear to me that another book was also asking to be written—inspired by John—but wholly focused on how civil disobedience can be used by Christians in this age of climate crisis. And so this is a kind of parallel text to John's, written from the perspective of an elderly Anglican priest, living and praying and taking action within the UK and as part of the UK based organisation, Christian Climate Action. I hope it will find a use as a further application of John's work, within the different social and political context of twenty-first century UK.

In 1990, John wrote:

> God is constantly at work in us and in our world, bringing forth God's reign of justice and peace on earth, here and now, as it is in heaven. Nonviolent civil disobedience is one way for us to cooperate with God's nonviolent, loving transformation of our world. When nonviolent civil disobedience is enacted in the Spirit of God's love, it can be a force for the transformation

> of the world. When it touches the spiritual streams of God's nonviolent love, when it is an act of obedience to the God of nonviolent love, it becomes sacramental.[1]

Since these words were written, the climate and ecological emergencies have taken centre stage in the world. It is clear that we are staring into the face of an abyss, with less than 10 years at most to turn things round—and this is an optimistic estimate of our chances. In 2018, Extinction Rebellion, beginning in the UK, broke through the wall of silence. The movement spread in a matter of months through Europe and on to the States, Asia and Australia. In Sweden, the teenager Greta Thunberg caught the world's attention with her uncompromising message that the older generation was stealing her future and this inspired school strikes and Fridays for the Future, to drive home the message that action on the climate was needed *now*.

It was the peace movement which had provided the crucible for many Christians and others, both in Europe and the US, to learn about civil disobedience and to apply some of the learning that had taken place during the abolition of slavery in the US and Britain; the Civil Rights movement in America; the struggle for independence in India; the suffragette movement in the US and Europe; and more recently, the anti-apartheid struggle in South Africa.

All were characterised by the ambition to remain nonviolent, even if this was not always entirely possible in practice. Likewise, the peace movement, by its very nature, was and is characterised by nonviolence because of the internal logic of the cause that it espouses. Now Christians are hearing the call anew to step up to the plate and confront governments with the radical nonviolent action that is required, if we are not to condemn practically all life on earth to extinction.

Ideas for this book have emerged from the rich interchanges that we often have within Christian Climate Action—at our daily meetings for prayer and chat, and at our various discernment and teaching meetings. I am indebted to my fellow members of CCA for these. When I am aware of its origin, I obviously attribute an idea to its author. Where I am not, I apologise. I have been helped in my thinking by participating in a course run by Green Christian called "Cloud and Fire" exploring the spirituality needed in order to ground our active work for the climate crisis.

I am also fed by the worship and teaching at my parish church and supported by its strong commitment to care for God's creation. I have many good friends who pray for me regularly whom I couldn't do without at all. More recently, my conversations and actions—taken as part of the Insulate Britain and Just Stop Oil Campaigns—have provided many new insights, relationships, conversations and experiences of civil disobedience. To all of these many friends and mentors I give great thanks.

But most of all, I owe the greatest debt to my dear friend Ruth Jarman, information officer at Green Christian as well as a founder member of CCA. She and I have been close companions on many actions and she has made it possible, by her practical help, for me to join in, even when sometimes feeling I might be too old to do so! She has meticulously sifted through the text and given me invaluable advice on many aspects of the subject, especially the science.

I want to thank Chris Donald, the editor, for all his helpful guidance and advice and my friend Ann Miller for undertaking the copy editing as an act of love! I hope that this book will be helpful in our shared task of obeying God's call.

**—Sue Parfitt, 2023**

# FOREWORD

It's a beautiful summer day as I sit down to write this along the Central Coast of California; sunny, but hot, very hot—around 40 °C. A couple of hours from here, in a place called Death Valley, the hottest temperature ever recorded in history will be reached this afternoon —55 °C. This past week has seen the hottest temperatures ever. The announcer on last night's National Public Radio news put it this way—"the hottest temperatures not just in a thousand years, but in tens of thousands of years."

We are getting used to reports like this. Hurricanes, tornadoes, wildfires, rain bombs, flooding, droughts, blizzards, heat domes—they are the new normal. A few months ago, the coldest place on earth—Antarctica—hit 21 °C. As I write, this year is on track to be the warmest year in the history of planet Earth. The dramatic, catastrophic warming of the planet is the inevitable result of using fossil fuels, which release heat into the atmosphere and oceans, raising the temperature and the ocean levels on the way toward the extinction of millions of species, who knows how many new wars and millions of unjust deaths by the end of the century.

We can no longer stop global warming, but we might be able to head off the worst of its effects. That demands urgent action from every one of us. Greta Thunberg is right: the planet is burning and we have to act like our house is on fire, because it is. That means, we have to drop what we are doing, stop the fire, make sure everyone is safe and help everyone and everything recover.

Just before the global pandemic hit, a call went out from actor Jane Fonda, Greenpeace, and key US environmentalists: calling for waves of civil disobedience aimed at the US Congress; a concerted demand for immediate action to stop the fossil fuel industry. Overnight, a grassroots movement launched called "Fire Drill Fridays."

The Friday I joined, a thousand of us marched on the US Capitol for a rally where we heard from indigenous women, youth, celebrities, and movement leaders calling for drastic action for climate justice. Then several hundred of us walked into the main US Senate office building and did what people have been doing across the world: we sat down, started singing, and refused to budge. We put our bodies on the line.

So much for business as usual. The building was shut down, and because there was a large open-air foyer and atrium that reached some ten stories high to the ceiling, hundreds of senate office workers looked down from their balconies to see what all the fuss was about.

One by one we were arrested, handcuffed, booked, fingerprinted, and bused to a nearby jail yard where we were held until midnight. We expected to be in the doghouse through the weekend, but, in my experience, police get tired of all that singing and good cheer and nonviolent resistance, and like a passage from the Acts of the Apostles, we were let out unharmed.

Strangely, we should have been dour and depressed, but the community spirit and willingness to risk jail and prison on behalf of creation and for disrupting US government business lifted our spirits and gave us hope.

History has shown us that, in the end, the only way positive social change ever happens is through bottom-up, people-power, grassroots movements of active, creative nonviolence; and that the turning point requires people on the front lines of these movements to put their bodies on the line and engage in civil disobedience.

This is a long noble tradition—from Jesus and St. Paul and the early church to the Abolitionists and Suffragists, to Gandhi and India's independence movement to Martin Luther King, Jr. and the US Civil Rights movement, and the countless grassroots movement since. When good people break bad laws which legalise systemic injustice, warfare, nuclear weapons, corporate greed, racism, and environmental destruction—and nonviolently accept the consequences of their actions—then positive change happens. In those tipping point moments, nonviolence becomes contagious.

But now we are faced with something none of us ever imagined: the breakdown of climate systems, and a permanent climate chaos that will bring many more wars, injustices, disasters, droughts, migrations, and deaths. On March 20, 2023, the Intergovernmental Panel on Climate Change, the United Nations group of climate experts, issued its most comprehensive report to date on catastrophic climate change, declaring that we have until the year 2030 to stop the ever-rising global average temperature at the 2015 Paris Climate agreement target of 1.5°C above preindustrial levels. Once that threshold is reached, there is no going back. Heat waves, flooding, drought, crops failures, arctic meltdowns, loss of coral reefs, and species extinction will be uncontrollable.

Yet despite the scientific evidence, the world's superpowers refuse to radically alter "business as usual." We would have to cut greenhouse gases at least by half by 2030 and stop adding carbon dioxide to the atmosphere completely by 2050, according to the report. Only then, might we have a 50 percent chance of limiting warming to 1.5°C.

The only way we will meet these goals is if people around the world rise, in the largest bottom-up, people-power global grassroots movement of creative nonviolence in the history of the world, and demand immediate action to stop the fossil fuel industries and force all governments to take immediate steps to prevent the most extreme catastrophes that lie ahead.

As I read such horrifying reports, I recall the words of Martin Luther King, Jr., offered the night before his assassination on April 3, 1968. "It's no longer a choice between violence and nonviolence," he said. "It's nonviolence or non-existence." In other words, unless the whole human race disarms, adopts the way of nonviolence, mobilises its people power political will to end greenhouse gas emissions, militarism, and environmental destruction—we are heading toward our own global destruction.

The good news, however, is that the end is not yet, that we do have a way forward, we are not powerless; we have power—the practice and methodology of organised, grassroots, active nonviolence as taught by Jesus, Gandhi, and Dr. King. If we mobilise together in global grassroots movements to demand immediate action, we can perhaps halt the worst of climate chaos. But that means, of course, we have to join the movement, and do our part in keeping the movement moving. As Archbishop Oscar Romero said the day he was assassinated, "No one can do everything, but everyone can do something!" Every one of us is needed. Every one of us has something to contribute.

My friend Sue Parfitt has been speaking out and taking action for years to protect Mother Earth and creation. A true disciple and prophet of the nonviolent Jesus, she continues to step up to the plate, call for dramatic public action, and cross the line in nonviolent civil disobedience to get the nations to stop "business as usual" and halt greenhouse gas emissions.

In this urgent and compelling book, Sue outlines how we can take action and put our bodies on the line to defend Mother Earth and creation. She issues the call, shares the way of active nonviolence from Jesus and the early church to today's young climate activists, and points out a path forward for each one of us.

More and more of us will have to put our bodies on the line like Sue Parfitt and get arrested and jailed in nonviolent resistance to stop big business and government inaction which is destroying Mother Earth.

In the end, Sue reminds us Christians that the best way we can help protect creation is through our participation in the paschal mystery of the nonviolent Jesus. She is telling us an ancient story: that the Gospel way of truth, justice and social change is the way of the cross, that each one of us is called to take up the cross of nonviolent resistance to the fossil fuel industry and their governments and corporations which continue to destroy creation. In doing so, we put our bodies on the line as Jesus did, and share in God's methodology of nonviolent risk and action that leads to the breakthrough of resurrection—when we finally transform the way we treat Mother Earth and one another, and create a more just, more nonviolent, more sustainable world.

If we rise to the occasion, step up and cross the line, we may be able to lead humanity back from the brink of destruction and non-existence, as Dr. King called us, and in doing so, we may be blessed with a renewed humanity and hope. As Dr. King said the week he was killed, in the end, "hope is the final refusal to give up." Like Dr. King, Sue Parfitt urges us not to give up, not to give in to despair and powerlessness, but, instead, to take the urgent action that is required.

Together, we go forward in prayer and hope, one step at a time, crossing the line, putting our bodies on the line, letting the chips fall where they may, and trusting in the God of peace to guide us into the wisdom of peace with Mother Earth and one another.

May this inspiring book energise you and renew you to do your part in the growing global grassroots movement of nonviolence to save and protect creation, that we might prevent the worst from happening, heal the planet, become true disciples of the nonviolent Jesus and welcome God's reign of peace on earth.

**—John Dear**
**Big Sur, California, 2023**

*INTRODUCTION*

# A CLARION

"What you doin' there, grandma?"

I had just fastened my high-visibility vest and sat down on the road. I gripped the end of the "Just Stop Oil" banner now stretching across half of the road, near Baker Street Underground station. My teammates were in place.

I looked up to see a short, grey-haired woman in her sixties, of south Asian origin.

"Dangerous sitting on the road, grandma," she continued, not waiting for my answer. "Come on the pavement with me."

"That's kind," I said, "but I'm where I need to be. Do you have children?" My friend became thoughtful, as though I had led her into a profoundly complex, maybe tragic area.

"Ah yes, grandma—but are they children any more? Quite old now, you see." The motorists were beginning to honk their horns; pedestrians shouted abuse.

"Well maybe then you have grandchildren?" I tried to redirect the conversation back to the substantive point: "I'm doing it for them." There was a pause—but not a very long one. Quite quickly my friend grasped what I was saying.

"You sit in the road for *my grandchildren*?" Her face was incredulous, but now wreathed in smiles. "Grandma, I'm proud of you!"

Some months earlier, we had been sitting on the M25 with signs stretched across the carriageway saying "Insulate Britain." Messaging doesn't get much clearer than that. But drivers in the line of trucks, vans and cars had edged up to our feet, and they were unimpressed.

One of our team walked between the vehicles handing out leaflets, explaining why we were there.

A lorry driver towered above us, shouting at the leaflet distributor and the rest of us. The expletives were delivered at high volume, but then gradually began to lessen. We could see that our teammate was listening to him and speaking with him. After about five minutes, the lorry driver suddenly jumped out of his cab and shook our teammate's hand. "I get it mate, I get it. You're doing it for *my kids!*"

In the desperate times in which we live, many Christians—as well as those of other faiths and none—feel themselves increasingly called to "cross the line" into acts of law-breaking. In the light of the climate emergency, Christians are engaging in civil disobedience: against the government, the fossil fuel industry, the media, the courts complicit with government inaction; and against the Church itself, when it is shying away from giving a needful prophetic lead to the world.

We undertake this because we believe that this is the only way for us to achieve the radical shifts required in government policy—or, as far as Christians are concerned, to adequately obey what God requires of us, for the Kingdom to be established on earth in this time of climate emergency. It is to this Christian calling that this book is devoted: to explain why I—a retired psychotherapist and octogenarian priest—have been sitting in the road, along with many others, and to call others to consider their own response.

As we traverse the twenty-first century, it has become clear that we are confronted by the greatest crisis that the planet and its inhabitants have ever had to face. We are facing an existential crisis, the sixth mass extinction event on planet Earth: the only one to have occurred since the advent of humanity.

Moreover, all other lesser crises have become entwined and bound up with the climate emergency. Climate change is causing increases in tropical diseases; climate change is causing and exacerbating extremes of wealth and poverty; climate change is causing global temperatures to rise so that large tracts of the Earth's surface are becoming uninhabitable, leading to an exponential rise in the migration of peoples in search of somewhere to grow food and raise children.

Climate change is affecting natural habitats and ecosystems in a myriad different ways. Even subtle adjustments can have a profound impact on the species living within an ecosystem. Whilst the jury is still out as to the aetiology of the covid pandemic, a recent paper addressed the question as to whether climate change influenced the emergence, transmission, and expression of the COVID-19 Pandemic. The authors concluded that this is likely to have been the case in all three areas. They went on to surmise that "pandemics will be more frequent in the future and more severely impactful unless climate changes are mitigated."[1] Other scientific work has investigated the links between habitat destruction and the resulting greater proximity between different species, including humans, allowing for the easier transmission of viruses.[2] What we know for sure is that the pandemic itself created a severe disruption throughout the world; it gave us a foretaste of what social breakdown will be like as the climate crisis worsens.

The pandemic caused by the Covid19 virus revealed, as never before, immense social and economic inequalities at every level of society—from local communities to international relationships—and the obscene year-on-year increase in the wealth of the very rich. These inequalities, too, negatively impact the climate. Covid may have interrupted the conversation on the climate emergency, but it also provided a circuit breaker in terms of "business as usual," enabling people all over the world to experience something of what life could be like without its addiction to fossil fuels. This period presented us with many difficulties, but it also gave us opportunities to imagine a new future.

Nonetheless, governments seem unable to act as though the house is already on fire. Not only is this true of their destructive actions in continuing to support the fossil fuel industry, but also by their inactions. Inaction is harder to identify, and makes protest more complicated perhaps than the protest against weapons of mass destruction which has absorbed much of the energy of activists both in Europe and the USA until recently.*

If ever there was a moment in the history of humankind for the followers of Jesus to step up to the plate and rise to our responsibilities—this, I want to argue, is surely it. And indeed, this impending climate catastrophe, already leading to the breakdown of social structures in some parts of the developing world, has unsurprisingly inspired acts of nonviolent civil disobedience in response.

But regrettably, many efforts to seek concrete solutions to the environmental crisis have proved ineffective; not only because of powerful opposition, but also because of a quite extraordinary inertia. Obstructionist attitudes, even on the part of believers, can range from denial of the problem to indifference, nonchalant resignation or blind confidence in technical (or Divine) solutions.

We require a new and universal solidarity, as the bishops of Southern Africa have stated. Members of the Symposium of the Episcopal Conference of Africa and Madagascar (SECAM) have joined other faith-based and civil society actors in demanding that world "decision makers" act fast to address the climate change crisis, which they say is a "striking example of structural sin." They go on to say that everyone's talents and involvement are needed to redress the damage caused by human abuse of God's creation. All of us can cooperate as instruments of God for the care of creation, each according to his or her own culture, experience, involvements and talents.[3]

For some, this will involve civil disobedience. That does not mean

—

* Not that the weapons industry is not a significant contributor to the climate emergency. The making, renewing, testing and threatening the use of weapons of mass destruction entails the emission of vast amounts of pollutants, yet these are usually not counted in a country's carbon budget, nor indeed are any of the other emissions produced by the military in its different areas of activity.

law-breaking for all of us; but I believe it does for some. Why would a Christian break the law? Fundamentally, because we are following Jesus. Jesus put justice as an expression of love at the heart of His ministry and mission. His love and compassion for His people—and for all people—drew Him inexorably into a radical search for justice. Always nonviolent—because violence is incompatible with love—Jesus is our model for every expression of our Christian faith, and our model for resisting the evil and the injustices we are confronted with today.

We follow the prophetic Jesus in seeking God's will for the creation. We participate in His passion for justice: justice for those parts of the world most deeply affected by climate change yet having done least to cause it, and justice for the generations to come who will have no liveable future unless we act. And we follow Him when necessary into acts of civil disobedience.

Jesus says "I was born and came into the world for this one purpose, to speak about the truth"(John 18:37). Indeed, we say Jesus is the Truth. One would therefore expect His followers, in whatever endeavour they are engaged, to place a very high value on truth. It is certainly so for climate crisis resisters and especially so for Christians. Telling the truth about the climate crisis—and about the evil, destructive nature of the fossil fuel industry and agri-business—is an imperative.

For Christians, our understanding of the climate crisis, and what we decide to do about it, needs to be filtered through the lens of our Christian faith and an understanding of Jesus—His priorities, His mission and His call to His followers to be active in the world. This will lead us to ask what it is that God is calling His disciples to do in this time of climate crisis, now.

## SIX GIRAFFES

*Philip Dixon*

The world turned on its scorched axis
and burned up common things
like grass to the fourth year.
The roots were gone, the cattle
moved on, the fourth year running,

...

The humans too fell by the wayside,
seed for wide-feathered birds.
The earth was less hospitable each year,
merciless and scouring.
The devastation is illustrated
by an aerial shot, showing
the carcasses of six giraffes.
They lie horizontal as if they might be
walking still. Or a circle dance
for the long-legged, but stiff
and rather arthritic. We remember
their walk and canter, gangling
about on their stilts.
The Darwin stories, the need
to get high food to survive.
These six giraffes are laid low now.
The only routine they knew was to drink
from the reservoir, legs splayed.
And, in the attempt they made
they got stuck
in the dried-up mud.

Who can not be moved witnessing
these noble, angular creatures.
Six giraffes
laid out as in a medieval
dance of death.
...And here, the painful beauty
of this company of giraffes.
Foolish no doubt to imagine them
comforting one another
in their last breath.
But there is one laying its head
on the flank of another.
The heart-breaking sight seems
composed, touching the depths of us,
making connection with antique time.
Prehistoric. Our common story.
We ask forgiveness.
Our indifference
is part of the reason
they lie here.
The pathos of it,
the awful beauty.
Sorrow.
Lament.
These six giraffes.

*The earth is the Lord's, and everything in it.*
*The world and all its people belong to him.*
Psalm 24

*If we surrendered to Earth's intelligence, we*
*could rise up rooted, like trees.*
Rainer Maria Rilke

ONE

# A CRISIS UNLIKE ANY OTHER

What is it about this crisis which requires such a costly response? Answering this question means truly understanding our predicament—without the comfort blanket of denial.

Hardly a week goes by without a deluge of articles and stories about climate change—because hardly a week goes by without a new manifestation of extreme weather events: floods, fires and famines in new and unexpected places. Despite the voluminous literature, expert and popular on the subject, we all remain climate deniers. How can we not be? In fact, the more we allow ourselves to understand the reality of the predicament we are in, the more we need to put that reality to one side, in order to keep on functioning at all.

There is a distinction to be made, however, between the psychological and emotional need for everyone to 'deny' the full meaning of what we face, and the deliberate obfuscation by governments, corporations, and multinationals—supported by much of the media—intent upon their own survival, whatever the cost to the planet, driven by corporate greed.

For climate change awareness is hampered by the efforts of the fossil fuel industry with its huge, worldwide interests in oil, coal and gas; by their lobbyists, and by the newspaper industry in the UK, Europe, Australia and the States, who continue to undermine the truth of climate change. In doing so, they help governments to avoid taking the draconian measures required to stop developing new coal mines and oil fields, fracking for gas, or laying new pipe lines—or indeed expanding airports, motorways, high-speed trains and the weapons industry.

In 1968, the American Petroleum Institute commissioned a report from Stanford University which stated that significant changes in temperature would almost certainly occur by the year 2000, bringing about climatic changes.[1] The fossil fuel industry, having commissioned this report, not only ignored it, but set out on "a multi-million-dollar drive of obfuscation and denial," as academic Bill McGuire put it, "designed to sow confusion and undermine public confidence in climate science and stymie the need for urgent action to tackle global warming." [2]

In the 50 years since, the oil industry has been making over *three billion dollars a day* in pure profit, as a study published by the University of Antwerp revealed in 2022. It's hard to assimilate such a figure.* The analysis reveals that the wealth captured by petro-states and fossil fuel companies since 1970 is $52tn, providing the power, as the author Aviel Verbruggen points out, to "buy every politician and every system" in the world and to delay at every point the critically urgent action needed to address the climate crisis.[3]

Indeed, lobbyists for the fossil fuel industry are active on every level of engagement, including at the international process tasked with dealing with the problem, the Conferences of the Parties.† In this sense, it is hard to overestimate the power and influence of the fossil fuel industry, or its ability to disguise and transform its activities in such a way that the truth cannot be revealed or acted upon. This makes it necessary, sometimes, to step back and see, afresh, the scale of our crisis.

*

—

* The analysis is based on World Bank data and the author of the report is Prof Aviel Verbruggen, at some point a lead scientist on the IPCC.

† The annual Cop events that are designed to find international agreements for reducing and eliminating the use of fossil fuels which are responsible for the year on year rise in carbon emissions; see Afterword.

During those 50 years, my own climate awareness developed gradually—as it did for many others. In 1962, Rachel Carson published her seminal book *Silent Spring*.[4] I don't remember actually reading it—I was focused on other things at the time, being in my second year at University—but I was aware of its content, in a general sort of way.

The book documented the adverse effects of pesticides on the environment, and the way in which the chemical industry had sought to disguise these harmful effects from the public (what's new?). "Knowing what I know, there would be no future peace for me if I keep silent," Rachel wrote to her friend Dorothy Freeman just before the publication of *Silent Spring*.[5] She also quoted from the poem *Protest* by the 19th century American poet, Ella Wheeler Wilcox:

> To sin by silence, when we should protest,
> Makes cowards out of men. The human race
> Has climbed on protest. Had no voice been raised
> Against injustice, ignorance, and lust,
> The inquisition yet would serve the law,
> And guillotines decide our least disputes.
> The few who dare, must speak and speak again
> To right the wrongs of many.[6]

I remember being incredulous at the thought that there might be no more birdsong. I have vivid memories as a child of taking our beds downstairs to sleep in the garden, to better hear the first herald of the dawn chorus. My father recorded it with the greatest enthusiasm—it was, I remember, quite deafening! Yet he continued to spray his plants with DDT and roll his peas in red lead before planting, to keep the mice away.

However, *Silent Spring* did have a profound effect; and some of the most toxic chemicals in agricultural and horticultural use, including DDT, were banned.*

—

* Rachel Carson was an early prophet of the biodiversity crisis. A visionary of uncommon

Another landmark: in 1968, the Apollo 8 spacecraft, looking for a landing spot, circled the moon and took the first ever pictures of planet Earth from space. That first famous photo became known as "Earthrise." For the first time, we saw planet Earth as it really was—with all its beauty and fragility—an entity in its own right. We wondered at the precariousness of our earthly home, seeing its boundaries, sensing its limits.

So beauty and wonder took on new meaning, and became drivers of our desire to care for what we have. The following year, Apollo landed on the moon, taking human beings off planet Earth for the first time—making us into distant spectators of our earthly home. To paraphrase the words of one of the astronauts, we went into space to discover new worlds, and ended up discovering our own.

The developing climate science began to show how human activity had increasingly impacted on the environment from the industrial revolution of the mid-nineteenth century on, and scientists and social scientists suggested that we had entered a new era of existence on earth for which a new name was needed to reflect humanity's effect. So the term *anthropocene* entered our vocabulary.*

Now, at any given moment, 1,000 satellites are orbiting the earth, showing us our planetary home in intense and novel detail. We see how rivers and their tributaries fan out like branches on a tree; we marvel at their beauty and form. But these pictures also reveal how all is not well. The reality of Arctic melt was brought home to us in 2017 with pictures of a huge iceberg breaking away and floating free. The effects of long-term drought in parts of Africa show only

---

courage and persistence, she has recently been celebrated in a poem dedicated to her far-reaching legacy, composed by Neil Gaiman (see Chapter 9).

* The Anthropocene working group, made up of 34 geologists, has worked since 2009 to establish the Anthropocene. Whilst the location for an official birthplace of the era has been agreed (Crawford Lake in Ontario, Canada), the geologists have not yet picked a specific year for its beginning. It is likely to be in the early 1950's, a time of great acceleration in human industrialisation activities, spreading across the planet.

too graphically what is happening and the devastating effects on the creatures who live there. Aerial pictures of Ghana's Volta Delta recently showed how in the space of only four years, a well-grassed and wooded landscape became barren and lifeless.

Priest poet Philip Dixon captures the terrible poignancy of what that means in his poem, *Lament for Six Giraffes*, an extract from which preceded this chapter.[7]

Not only satellite and aerial information, but television has opened our eyes to the natural world. We learned the interconnectedness of the climate and biodiversity crises through the extraordinary revelations of David Attenborough's discoveries, and the continuing work of Chris Packham and other naturalists, first marvelling at the variety and beauty of all that God had made, and then becoming increasingly aware of all that we have lost. WWF's Living Planet Report 2022 reveals there has been a 69% drop in global wildlife populations since 1970, a staggering rate of decline. 96% of global mammal biomass is now either human or livestock—only 4% being wild mammals.[8]

Yet even as our awareness has grown, as a society we have failed to respond. An increasing volume of publications recognises that we have now wreaked as much damage on the earth knowingly than ever we had done out of our innocence. Journalist David Wallace-Wells, in his book *The Uninhabitable Earth*, explores the wide-ranging effects of this destruction: wildfires, ocean dying, air pollution, epidemics, floods, heat waves, economic and social collapse, migration of peoples and concludes that:

> [T]o the extent we live today under clouds of uncertainty about climate change, those clouds are projections not of collective ignorance about the natural world but blindness about the human one, and can be dispersed by human action. This is what it means to live beyond the "end of nature" — that it is human action that will determine the climate of the future, not systems beyond our control.[9]

It is now clear that five arenas of concern need urgent attention: climate change driven by continuous human induced global heating; the degraded condition of the earth's land surface; air pollution; biodiversity loss on land and in the oceans; waste, and especially plastic and sewage waste. Of these, the most pressing, urgent and immediate is climate change.

In the decades since the first UN COP Climate Change Conference in 1995, as Bill McGuire puts it, "we have used up an entire bale in prevarication and inertia, so all we are left to clutch is the last straw. We cannot fail to grasp it." McGuire traces the history of the awareness of the part played by carbon emissions in the heating of the planet* and identifies a woman, Eunice Foote, as the author of the first paper making this connection as far back as 1865.[10]

He charts the number of times that the IPCC has sounded the alarm since its inception: "We have been put on notice time and time again about the potentially catastrophic impact of rising greenhouse gas levels in the atmosphere, but we have repeatedly refused to listen and chosen not to act."[11]

McGuire's book *Hothouse Earth*, written before the dramatic climate events of 2022-23, made it clear that catastrophic climate change is happening faster than even the worst scientific predictions.

Johan Rockström, Director of the Potsdam Institute for Climate Action Research in Germany comments: "Without doubt, extreme weather events, amplified by global warming, are coming faster than predicted and are more severe than predicted. The impacts are there to see: the disastrous floods in Pakistan; the failure of the rainy season in Somalia for the past four years; and highly destructive wildfires in

—

* One might mention the revolution in the 1970s where the 'new physics' gave greater insight into the interconnectedness of everything, including how human beings impact their environment. In 1973 the Schumacher lectures spread the idea that *Small is Beautiful*, critiquing unlimited growth and the loss of the "tolerance margins which benign nature always provides." (**33**) In 1979, James Lovelock's Gaia hypothesis helped to heighten awareness of ecological concerns and climate science. (**34**)

California."[12] And all this is happening now, when temperatures since pre-industrial levels have risen by only 1.2 degrees.

It only gets worse. According to a UN report in October 2022, the earth is now on track for a 2.5 degree rise in global temperatures by the end of the century. Successive reports from the Intergovernmental Panel on Climate Change have demonstrated the continuous growth in carbon emissions* and the increasing warming of the planet. Conservative by nature, the IPCC's Sixth assessment of the state of climate change—the synthesis report—finally pulled no punches,† stating starkly that it was now not possible to limit global temperatures to 1.5 degrees or even 2 degrees. We shall be touching 3 degrees by the end of the century, when babies being born now will still be alive.[13]

Yet resistance to making the hard decisions that have to be made now seems only to increase, pressured by the fossil fuel industry and supported by the media; the *Telegraph* called the latest IPCC Report "confected hysteria."[14]

Rockström believes that the world is heading towards 2-3 degrees, beyond the point where a number of tipping points to irreversible warming may be breached. David Armstrong McKay, another author of the report, added: "We're not saying that, because we're going to hit some tipping points, everything is lost and it's game over.‡ Every

---

* Other emissions are also crucial in their effect on global warming, notably methane, much of which is emitted by the food and farming industries. So an urgent transition away from animal-based food to a more plant-based diet is required of us, moving in parallel with a reduction and elimination of fossil fuels.

† Eight years in the making, involving hundreds of experts, and signed off by nearly 200 governments, it represents the global consensus on the science of climate change. Its findings are unequivocal – that human-induced climate change has led us to the brink of catastrophe. Other major reports from the International Energy Authority and Chatham House published later in 2021 corroborated all that the IPCC had stated (**35**). These Reports show that since the publication of the first IPCC Report in 1990, total greenhouse gas emissions have risen by 43% and the atmospheric concentration of carbon dioxide has increased from 354ppm to 420ppm.

‡ Scientists now think that we are on the point of crossing five critical tipping points

fraction of a degree that we stop beyond 1.5C reduces the likelihood of hitting more tipping points."[15]

If that all feels abstract, what felt real to many was that the summer of 2022 was the hottest on record in the UK and in many other parts of the world. In the UK, temperatures topped 40 degrees for the first time ever. India experienced temperatures of over 50 degrees. Huge and deadly fires raged throughout Europe for weeks, which had its worst drought since the sixteenth century. Rivers dried up. Flash floods after the heatwaves brought destruction in many parts of the world. Sea level rises forced island dwellers to relocate.

The Horn of Africa saw its worst drought in forty years; several South American countries saw prolonged drought and crop failure whilst Pakistan experienced the worst monsoon floods ever, affecting every province in the country. North America had its second hottest July on record; and a record all-time low in Antarctic sea ice was observed.

Research by other scientists noted a major surge in methane being emitted, beginning in 2020 and continued into 2021: "If you think of fossil fuel emissions as putting the world on a slow boil, methane is a blow torch that is cooking us today," says Durwood Zaelke—President of the Institute for Governance & Sustainable Development, and an advocate of stricter policies to reduce methane emissions. "The fear is that this is a self-reinforcing feedback loop... If we let the earth warm enough to start warming itself, we are going to lose this battle."[16]

In a paper published in the Proceedings of the National Academy of Sciences, July 2022, researchers at the University of Cambridge, led by Dr Luke Kemp, called on the IPCC to dedicate a future report to the possibility of a "climate endgame" to galvanise research and inform the public. They proposed a research agenda for facing up to bad-to-worst case scenarios. These include outcomes ranging from a loss of 10% of the global population to eventual human extinction:

---

– points at which physical change becomes self-reinforcing and can no longer be stopped. Passing one tipping point is often likely to help trigger others, producing cascades.

"there are plenty of reasons to believe climate change could become catastrophic, even at modest levels of warming."[17]

The American Petroleum Institute's report made clear that almost everything we know now, we already knew in 1979, if not before.* Yet once we knew what we were doing, we did it all the more! Carmody Grey, a Roman Catholic theologian, asks why and points to one reason: perhaps the continuous release of shocking data about the planet actually makes matters worse.[18] The data becomes normalised within us and, as we look out onto our immediate world, things still look much the same as they always have, so the data gets assimilated into the psyche and kept at arm's length, no longer producing the shock to the system which it once might have done.

A further crucial reason for our inaction concerns our assumptions about the necessity for continuous economic growth. Economic growth is incompatible with reducing carbon emissions, yet the growth model continues to underpin the economic policies of all major economies. Naomi Klein quotes Yvo de Boer, "who held the UN's top climate position until 2009 and who remarked recently that 'the only way' negotiators 'can achieve a 3 degree goal is to shut down the whole global economy'." Klein goes on to say that although this is an overstatement, we cannot nevertheless achieve carbon cuts with the sort of modest carbon pricing or green tech solutions that are on the table.[19]

Emissions cuts above 1% "have historically been associated with economic recession or upheaval," as Nicholas Stern put it in his 2006 report to the UK government.[20] What national economy is going to invite that?

—

* In the words of family therapist Philip Kearney: "Gregory Bateson admonished us forty years ago that 'the unit of survival is organism plus environment... we are learning by bitter experience that the organism which destroys its environment destroys itself.' Bateson described 'chopping up the ecology' [ie not understanding the unbreakable interconnection of phenomena with their environment] as the most serious epistemological error." (**36**)

## THE PASTORAL CRISIS

Admittedly, for all of us, as each new report emerges from the IPCC, the IEA, Chatham House and from academic departments all over the world, so much bad news may feel overwhelming. How do we take in the truth of what science is telling us, and still go about our everyday lives?

If we did not deny what is happening to ourselves and our planet, at some level, how could we wake up each morning and go about the business of the day? How could we plan our future—even a short time ahead, or prepare our gardens for the coming year, or enter into courses of study or save up our money to buy our first home, let alone embark on parenthood and the care of a new generation?

Yet there comes a point where denial is impossible, and we must face the emotional consequences: which can mean grief, powerlessness, helplessness, and an unresolved sense of loss. "Climate anxiety" is becoming part of common discourse now; the many and frequent reports on the science of climate change make grim reading, and the American Psychology Association (APA) coined eco-anxiety as "the chronic fear of environmental cataclysm that comes from observing the seemingly irrevocable impact of climate change and the associated concern for one's future and that of next generations."[21]

But Caroline Hickman, working as a climate psychologist at the University of Bath, insists that climate anxiety—like climate depression—is not a pathology; it's a reasonable and healthy response to an existential threat. "I'd kind of wonder why somebody *wasn't* feeling anxious," she says. So the first step is to acknowledge the validity of these feelings. The job of a climate psychologist is then to ask: "How can we support you to make this part of your life and not all of your life?" Hickman continues: "Our children's anxiety is a completely rational reaction given the inadequate responses to climate change they are seeing from governments.* What more do governments need to hear to take action?"[22]

In the face of rising levels of eco-anxiety, the Royal College of Psychiatrists agrees with Hickman, stating eco-distress "is not a mental disorder... it should be considered a meaningful response to the ecological emergency."[23] Even so, as Professor McMichael in the *British Medical Journal* confirmed, there is a "clear relation between experiencing climate change effects and the increased risks of depression, low mood, extreme mental distress, post-traumatic stress disorder, suicide, and further deterioration in those with a history of mental illness."[24]

This has a disproportionate impact on children and the young: Rao and Powell cite evidence that child psychiatrists in England are finding distress about the climate crisis is apparent in over half of the children referred to them.[25]

Surveys have found this to be true in other countries too; climate anxiety is "profoundly affecting huge numbers of these young people around the world," and especially those in the global south. Rao and Powell again make the significant comment that this "is the first study to offer insights into how young people's emotions are linked with their feelings of betrayal and abandonment by governments and adults. Governments are seen as failing to respond adequately, leaving young people with "no future" and with "humanity doomed."[26]

"Waking up to the reality of climate change is very similar to bereavement," argues therapist Rosemary Randall:

> ...only with a death, there is a set of rituals to follow, rules of behaviour to guide others and public acknowledgement of your status as bereaved. But if you are facing grief about climate change, you are among people who are as distressed as you, or people who can't understand why you are upset. And if you

—

* Hickman goes on to encourage patients to join an activist group, or a discussion and support group like a climate cafe—a point I will return to.

> see a therapist who doesn't get it, you are being injured again. It is a form of disenfranchised grief.[27]

When these complex feelings become unmanageable and no recourse can be found internally within the psyche or externally within the social support system of family, friendship group or activist network, the ultimate choice may be to end one's life. The unbearable pain of facing the truth; the fear of having to accept penalties which take one beyond what can be endured.

Research into the connection between suicide and eco despair is scant at present, but I have seen how this event, occurring within the tightly formed network of an activist group, impacted on climate activists, as well as on the individual's own family. Beyond the obvious feelings of sadness, guilt and bereavement, were overlaid questions about the ultimate purpose of the protest actions, a sense of depression about their effectiveness and the seemingly hopeless situation we are in—all of which needed working through, within the group and on an individual level, with the help of counsellors. The experience led me to ponder further how much more difficult our present predicament is for the young, and therefore for the young activist.*

The climate crisis is inescapable for the young. And for young activists in their twenties and thirties, it must be hard to imagine that there is going to be any normal life at all—because of the crisis itself, and because of one's commitment to the endless cycle of actions, arrests, trials and imprisonment. Yet how to get off this treadmill and still remain true to one's beliefs and make a meaningful difference? How to accommodate such an unknowable future?

The field of psychology itself is having to adapt to address these

---

* For older people, the future may look bleak but it is not going to last forever! And a lot of living has already been done while we were still in that age of innocence as to the effects of burning fossil fuels.

experiences. The skills of psychotherapists and counsellors are needed to hold and transform the grief and fear that is already manifesting in consulting rooms. In confronting the rising anxiety, Cohen and her colleagues argue that coaching (and counselling) as a whole needs a transformation of focus: "from self to system, individual to community and growth to restoration. Many coaches do work systemically, but there are also many working only with the client in the room."[28]

Family therapy is a methodology that helps therapists to move into this arena: beyond the individual and his or her pathology, and into the connections between the individual and his or her environment. Nearly 50 years ago, in 1976—following the innovative work of American family therapists—I wrote about these interconnections: not understanding at the time the full significance of the insights that flow from this method of work; or how vital such an understanding would become in our present dire predicament.[29] Other family therapists have endorsed this view very recently.[30]

Family therapists may have a particular role to play in helping activists and their families with the fundamental difficulty of contradictory impulses: the urgent need to try to intervene in the crisis and bring about change, on the one hand; and the simultaneous need to find ways of adapting and living in the situation we are in, which maybe cannot be changed very much.

This fundamental contradiction is often played out within the activist's family. One partner joins a radical protest group and is arrestable; the other repudiates all direct action, believing it to be useless, counterproductive and deeply harmful to their relationship and to other members of the family. One partner becomes clinically depressed; the other is able to disown their depression by plunging into action.

Or the adult children in the family feel embarrassed and distressed by their parent's appearances in court and in the newspapers. They react with hostility, or with a silent emotional cut off.

Or the young children in the family are suffering from eco-anxiety because of what they are hearing about the climate crisis in school or talked about at home. They become school-phobic or aggressive towards their parents or siblings.

By inviting the couple or family group to come together and talk about their concerns—their anger, shame and fear—together with a therapist, it may be possible in quite a straightforward way to help everyone to understand each other's choices better, as well as own feelings that have become projected onto others and unhelpfully disowned.

"Each generation of activists thinks they just need to tell the truth and tell it louder, but people are just as likely to shoot the messenger as listen," write Randall and Hoggett. The Climate Psychology Alliance has developed workshops called *Taking the heat out of talking about climate change* aimed at helping people have what Randall and Hoggett call "everyday conversations with friends, family and colleagues who are ambivalent about climate change." They are "what we all do every day as psychotherapists with clients who come to us desperately wanting to change, but also wanting things to remain the same."

They argue that despair and depression are a necessary fuel for action:

> What happens when we think about climate change is that part of us hears what people are saying about the implications and part of us can't believe it will actually come to pass, so we just don't think about it; we close off. Or we split thoughts from feeling; we allow ourselves to think the thoughts but not to feel the feelings that should go with it. So we are left with the facts but not the emotional response that would make us do something about it. That is what emotions do—they fuel our actions in a way that simply intellectually knowing doesn't, because facts don't disturb. So you have to stay with that disturbance and that is the difficult thing—the ability to park it on one side and get on with what you do. That is what activists

> and scientists can do, as our survey showed. It's not denial or disavowal; it's not lying. It actually frees you to act. **31**

Anger, too, is an important and frequent response to increased climate awareness; anger experienced by those who believe in the reality of the climate crisis, and the anger of those who do not. Even weather forecasters have reported increasing hostility from climate deniers when they link extreme weather events with climate breakdown, complaining of scaremongering.*

Anger and rage is a rational response to what has been done, to what has already been destroyed, and to the continuous process of destruction that goes on around us—even though we now know what is happening, and why. Anger at deforestation as it continues at pace, removing the green lungs of the planet at a speed which cannot be matched by the many rewilding and reforestation initiatives, however well-intentioned. Anger at all the broken promises of COP26 and 27 and the great U-turns of our government, and those of others in their decisions to excavate for new fossil fuels: oil, gas and coal. Rosebank is the biggest undeveloped oil field in the UK and, at the time of writing, awaits the Government's decision to allow its development, almost certainly to be granted, despite Government commitment to reduce drastically carbon emissions from fossil fuels.

To be a Christian at this time demands that we review the imperatives of our faith, against the challenges placed upon it, within the particular circumstances in which we are living. As Pope Francis† says, attending to the climate crisis is not some add-on extra in which

---

* I would argue that meteorologists play an important role in communicating climate change to the public, especially in the face of a refusal by much of the media to tell the truth about what the science is telling us.

† In 2015, Pope Francis published his encyclical *Laudato Si'*. Like no other papal encyclical before, the influence of *Laudato Si'* has been immense and spread far beyond the confines of the Christian Church. In it, Pope Francis linked the cry of the earth with the cry of the poor, and placed the needs of climate justice—for those suffering most now, and for future generations—firmly on the agenda.

a Christian might choose to engage, but a central requirement of our faith.[32] Likewise, care of the planet is one of the five marks of mission observed by the Anglican Church. It is God's planet; God is its Creator, and climate justice for the planet itself—for Mother Earth, and for her peoples and creatures—is central to Christianity.

Ultimately, the inhabitants of our planet—human, animal and plant—are being destroyed by the corporate greed of the rich and powerful, and by the thoughtless selfishness of us all. We need, as Pope Francis has said, an eco-conversion which opens our eyes to what we have done, and which helps us to commit ourselves to living sustainably, gently and lightly upon the earth—now, and in the future. We need to create the conditions for mutual respect and equality between peoples, and between the human and non-human species on the planet, so that we begin to understand that this is the only way we can survive and flourish on the Earth, in the way that God always intended.

The response to the crisis by the population at large and by the governments of the world is wholly inadequate. Fear, denial, paralysis, greed, cowardice, self-interest is preventing humanity doing what it needs to do: that is, to stop burning fossil fuels, refuse to extract new ones from the ground, stop deforestation, the keeping of animals for food and the pollution of sea, rivers and air. God needs people as never before to address this crisis, and to do what needs to be done, whatever the cost to themselves. God needs them to give the whole of themselves to the task of restoring, caring for and preserving the beautiful creation that God has made.

God needs the followers of Jesus to pit themselves against the violence and evil of the fossil fuel industry, and the exploitative and corrupt political and monetary systems by which we are governed, and enable their power to be overcome with God's nonviolent love. God needs the Church, in all its forms, to stand up and cry from the housetops that we have to follow the science and do what needs to be done. In other words, God needs the Church to be prophetic; to call out evil, and to lead people into the ways of justice, truth and peace.

## RUTH JARMAN

I sit cross-legged, cushioned from the tarmac by a garden kneeler, my vulnerability protected by the lines of orange-hi-vis-clad warm-hearted humans sitting to my right and left across the entrance to Kingsbury Oil depot. In front of me a line of policemen in black and yellow, guarding a backdrop of squat white concrete vats of the shiny liquid that both maintains our civilisation and will destroy it. I wonder how they feel about their job protecting this site from us, 51 ordinary people, armed with no more than knowledge and integrity, here to protect life.

I sing the Taize song *O Lord hear my prayer*, quietly. I feel alive. This is my prayer—just being at this place at this time with these people.

The Pixy vans start arriving. A rather nervous policeman, not much older than my teenage son, reads the injunction and asks me if there is anything he can do to get me to move. My suggestion that he joins Just Stop Oil is not taken seriously and I am soon sitting in the comfort of a police car driving to Nuneaton Police Station. I was later pleased to read an excellent précis of our conversation in my arresting officer's witness statement: 'She stated that something had to be done in order to start change within the world and this was why she believed that protesting and breaching the injunction was necessary.'

*God in His mercy has given us this work to do*
*and so we are not discouraged.*
2 Cor. 4:1

*Lo I come, to do Thy Will oh my God.*
Psalm 40

*TWO*

# FAITH, SPIRITUALITY AND SOLIDARITY

As people of faith, we understand that this is God's planet, God's creation, and that we are entrusted by God for its care and protection. We believe that God loves, with an infinite love, every tiniest creature that God has made, and grieves with unutterable grief for the pain and distress experienced by the least of God's creatures. We are therefore able to invoke a *reason beyond ourselves*, and our own self-care, for the actions that we take to protect it.

As God's children, brought into being by Love and upheld by God's care, we are impelled out of a reciprocal love for God to do all that we are able to do, to protect and cherish all that God has made.

More broadly, the climate crisis is a spiritual crisis. Stephen Wright and Cat Jenkins, of the Deep Adaptation Forum, write that "the possibility of environmental and social collapse is a fearful prospect... this is the very stuff of spirituality, and a spiritual crisis needs spiritual solutions as well as social, economic, emotional and ecological ones." [1]

The *deep adaptation* that is their organisation's namesake is something we will need to move towards: the process of finding new ways to live in solidarity with one another, perhaps in intentional communities. Jem Bendell, a founder member of the Forum, believes that we do a disservice to our congregations if we do not face up to the likelihood of societal collapse with them. [2]

The Deep Adaptation Forum, then, focuses on developing ways in which we might respond to this reality. They propose ways forward: facing the truth, building resilience and developing relationships of mutual support, with faith groups playing an important role.*

Acknowledging the reality of where we are in the flow of climate events does not mean activism has no further part to play; but activism needs to go alongside the effort to live authentically, responsibly and even joyfully in the 'now' of what is happening. Whether the commitment to build alternative communities of sustainable living, in fact, saps the energy out of active protest has yet to be tested. But it seems that this need not be so.†

Joanna Macy and Chris Johnstone—whose book, *Active Hope*, has the subtitle *How to face the mess we're in without going crazy*—write from a Buddhist perspective.They itemise four positions which can help us: *gratitude*, *honouring our pain*, *seeing with new eyes* and *going forth*.[3] Taking time each day to review what it is that we are grateful for and giving thanks for every bit of it; allowing the pain of the world to flood into our being rather than resisting it so that our capacity for compassion is expanded; seeing beyond ourselves as individuals and instead, realising our connectedness with all other living creatures and the earth itself (an idea explored many years earlier by anthropologist Gregory Bateson, called "the pattern that connects")[4] and finally, going forth into action, led by a vision that inspires us.

In order to move through this sequence, Macy and Johnstone suggest that we need to develop belief that our vision is possible, building support around it to maintain energy and momentum which then leads to active hope. Macy and Johnstone are completely realistic that we are probably heading for the endgame of our civilisation, yet "the process of turning up to play our part, turning towards our hopes

—

* DAF's website states that: "when using the term social or societal collapse, we are referring to the uneven ending of our current means of sustenance, shelter, security, pleasure, identity and meaning." (**14**)

† However, looking at this from the other way round, to be continuously committed to "rage, rage against the dying of the light" might make for uncomfortable living in community!

and turning away from behaviours that make our fears more likely is something we can do from any starting point. We live at a time when the stakes are so high, when so much rests on what we do."[5] As Greta Thunberg says, "it's never too late to do as much as we can."[6]

## A CHRISTIAN RESPONSE

A Christian response to the climate crisis is to dig deep into our store of faith and belief, and apply it to the crisis and to the many ways in which people are trying to cope with it. In so doing, Christians can contribute to helping manage the painful and very difficult feelings that will increasingly confront us all. Christians have been in the forefront of sounding the alarm about the climate crisis and leading a response. Notably, Bill McKibben, the Methodist activist and writer in the United States—founder of the environmental groups 350.org and The Third Act—has given a powerful lead.[7]

For Christians, nothing can be accomplished without prayer—intercessory prayer, and the deeper contemplative prayer of silence that enables us to do the work of God, rather than acting out of the needs of our own egos. Contemplative prayer enables God, not us, to lead the way. Without deep, consistent prayer, the activist can begin to believe that s/he has the ability to make things happen and to change evil into good and then to become discouraged when these efforts fail.

Likewise, political action is essential, but it can become divorced from the needs of real human beings unless it is rooted in day-to-day contact with those who suffer. Political activism needs grounding in the realities of the lives of those who have little power to change their circumstances and needs to be done as far as possible *alongside* rather than *on behalf of* them. Political action will thus ideally be linked with pastoral care. Both need to be rooted in prayer, and all of these activities will hopefully have a prophetic dimension as they call other Christians, and many others outside the faith, into attending to the needs of a suffering and unjust world.

For Christians, prayer helps us be divested from our own pride, egotism, greed, inertia, violence, cowardice and self-seeking, and to be conformed to the pattern of God's justice and love as it is revealed in Jesus. All of this helps us cope with our feelings and our fears, as it re-directs our energy into positive decisions about what we can do to help others and Mother Earth.

Prayer; personal spiritual development; pastoral care; political action and prophecy are the building blocks of Christian life. Every Christian is called to engage in them all. They depend upon one another.

As we respond to the impending climate catastrophe, there is thus a role for every Christian to play their part. There is no hierarchy involved in the different kinds of action which Christians are called to undertake. Nonviolent direct action and civil disobedience are not morally superior to other Christian responses to the crisis. All Christians are expected to give the *whole* of themselves in response to whatever calling they are given, and that remains true of our calling to be responsive to the climate emergency.

For example, climate change will soon be—maybe already is—the biggest driver of migration, and migrants from the global south are already seeking re-location in those parts of the world not yet seeing the worst effects of change.[8] So asylum seekers and refugees seeking a new home will need welcome, care and hospitality as well as advocacy with governments for their human rights to be acknowledged and fulfilled.

Again, the indigenous peoples in north America, in the Amazon and many parts of Africa will be subject to fiercer and fiercer pressure to give up their land to the fossil fuel extractors and to the industrial meat producers, and will need advocacy from those of us able to put pressure on our governments to offer them protection. Indigenous peoples throughout the world are the original protectors of the land

and its creatures, and they have everything to teach those of us who have only so much more recently become aware of our responsibilities.

All of these issues of justice are interconnected, and all of them now relate to the one overarching issue of climate change and climate injustice and require from us a response commensurate with the demands of our Christian faith.

I return to the poem, *Lament for Six Giraffes* by Philip Dixon, quoted before Chapter 1. Contemplating such a scene, we may be drawn to pray in humility for ourselves, for the fossil fuel industry and the banks that support it, for the agri business, for the governments of the world, for the judges and the courts, for the weapons industry, for the super rich, for all humanity...

*Kyrie eleison, Christi eleison, Kyrie eleison.*

We are beginning to understand only too clearly that it is we, ourselves, who are responsible and that, however much we try to lower our carbon footprint now, we are profoundly culpable personally as well as politically for the destruction we have already caused and continue to cause. There is an important role for penitence in helping us all to manage our depression, anxiety and fear and to move into action. Penitence and the desire to make reparation help us change ourselves and our own destructive behaviour and free us in turn to become more effective agents of change.

Penitence brings us face to face with reality and helps us shoulder our own responsibility; it helps us live in the real world and saves us from wasting time and energy on blaming others for what has happened. Penitence is what leads us to *metanoia*—a turning—a fundamental and deep-seated change in an individual's direction and perspective. Metanoia leads us to the conversion of heart which in turn opens our eyes to the evil in which we have participated and the good which beckons us instead into new life. We need our lives to be transformed at a deep level by the workings of God's grace.

Perhaps most obviously, *every* Christian is called to attend to and make the necessary changes in our own lifestyle in response to the urgent need to care for Mother Earth. Christians in the rich global north have to face up to the fact that, however poor we may be—and even in this time of austerity—we live, with very few exceptions, in total luxury compared with many in the global south, where climate change is a very present reality already severely impacting other pre-existing conditions of poverty and deprivation.

For us who are so privileged, learning to do *without*, learning to have *less*, learning to consume *little*, learning to waste *nothing*, will *not* in itself interrupt the impending climate catastrophe. It is simply the right way to live and an important way to love our neighbour at this time. It also helps us to be more authentic and less prone to the charge of hypocrisy when we take wider action. We can all do something—whether it be learning to live with less white washing; less warm homes; less well-watered gardens or making changes in our diet so as to reduce or eliminate animal foodstuffs altogether.

When so many go short of food in the world, some sacrificial acts are both necessary and meaningful. Sacrifice will indeed be increasingly required, and Christians of all people ought to be able to give the lead to others in this respect. Sacrifice motivated by love is at the heart of our faith, and it may be that our understanding of what this entails is one of the gifts we have to offer to others at this time.

## CHRISTIAN CLIMATE ACTION

Christian Climate Action provides an obvious home for Christians within the climate protest movement. CCA came into being in the UK in 2012. A group of friends from different Christian denominations, who had all been working for some years in environmental organisations and involved in protest, saw the need for a group which would enable and support Christians who felt called to undertake nonviolent direct action and civil disobedience as part of their commitment of faith.[9]

The group was committed to bringing climate change to the

forefront of the minds of governments, churches and ordinary citizens and telling the truth about the climate crisis. It was also committed to taking nonviolent direct action to highlight the crisis and engaging in acts of civil disobedience leading to arrest, trial and imprisonment.

In 2014, prayers were said by CCA members outside Downing Street, when the Prime Minister, David Cameron, was refusing to attend an international climate summit. Two octogenarians, Reggie Norton and Phil Kingston, knelt down and prayed, blocking the entrance to Downing Street, for 30 minutes. Others stood near, said prayers and sang hymns. Other early actions consisted in white-washing the walls of the Department for Energy and Climate Change and renaming it the 'Department for Extreme Climate Change' on the first day of the Paris climate conference in 2015. In April 2019, the group received the backing of the former Archbishop of Canterbury, Dr Rowan Williams, who said Christian Climate Action was responding to the scale of our environmental crisis.

> Christians are called by God to show to the world what the divine image looks like—the image of a divine creator who brought the world to birth, called it good, and summoned human beings to reflect this divine care and delight through their own work in the world, animated by the gift of Christ's Spirit. Christian Climate Action seeks to respond to that summons; in the face of impending environmental crisis, we need to encourage one another to grow more fully into the joyful responsibility we are made for.[10]

CCA would eventually become the Christian wing of Extinction Rebellion (XR), after that new movement emerged in the autumn of 2018.* Many now find their spiritual home in XR, whose principles

---

* These kinds of coalitions are commonplace: two leading members of that group, Roger Hallam and Gail Bradbrook, have gone on to shape the movement in different ways since its inception, and new developments and coalitions have taken place adapting to the changing urgency and need as it is presented by the crisis. Roger Hallam,

are strong and entirely compatible with the Christian faith. Others find their support group amongst like-minded people in their church. Some are finding it mainly within Christian Climate Action itself.

As we move more deeply into this crisis, a support group will be an important and necessary part of what will sustain a long-term commitment to this struggle. We will need to build resilience, endurance and strength but also grow in freedom, detachment and vision and the ability to discern God's will and the part God wants us to play in bringing it about. Several courses have been developed by Green Christian to help Christians in their response to the climate crisis and to help them support others in parishes and beyond.*

As the realities of climate change take root in people's minds, we shall need to learn to care for each other in new ways and build solidarity and community. Christians will be needed to take a lead in offering pastoral care and succour to those who enter the shadowlands of despair and mental breakdown, and find new ways of responding to the spread of mental distress, anxiety and fear.

An important further question to explore, I would add, is how the climate crisis impacts *our own* faith. There seems to have been little, if any, research into this question. Yet the question as to whether the crisis engenders a firmer faith, or makes faith in a loving God difficult or impossible, is obviously a highly relevant matter. We must speak the truth to ourselves as well as to others; and this involves facing up to the likelihood that we have indeed left it too late to avert the

---

for example, has been instrumental in the formation of the radical campaigns Insulate Britain, Just Stop Oil and Burning Pink.

* Green Christian came into being in 1981 to offer this help as well as to share knowledge and provide insights about climate change to Christians in the wider Church community. Through initiatives such as its Way of Life group, it offers support, ideas and teaching as to how to live gently on the earth, cope with the emotional stress of facing up to the climate crisis and practise a Rule of Life to sustain us in our commitment to engage with the crisis through action and prayer. The Way of Life Rule is fourfold and involves daily prayer, public witness, mutual encouragement and living gently upon the earth.

climate catastrophe, even if some of its worst effects can still be mitigated.

## SOLIDARITY WITH ONE ANOTHER

We need to build an inclusive movement which has room for everyone, whatever their background, identity, talents and limitations of time or work and family responsibilities. This is no time to deny to others the strengthening support that we gain from being part of a group. This requires sensitivity and skill, especially as the climate coalition of resistance gets bigger and more diverse and the climate crisis becomes ever more urgent.

I have heard the majority white, middle class, professional climate protest movement lamenting the lack of BAME participation. This overlooks the fact that minority groups in society may pay a disproportionately high cost for their involvement in protests and, if taking part in arrestable action, may attract a much more adverse response from police and prison authorities.

These groups—and likewise the LGBT community—have also felt angry and marginalised at times, by the white-led climate movement's expression of overriding urgency and determined mobilisation, which seemed to mirror too closely the imperialist, excluding dominance under which people of colour and people of differing sexual identities live.

Opportunity for gentle discussion, reflection and mutual learning is needed in order to hear and really listen to the anxieties and anger of people who, as well as coping with their anxiety about the climate crisis, may feel rejected or ignored when offering their gifts to the climate movement and deeply afraid about the consequences of doing so.

Likewise, people with major work or family responsibilities may feel that because they are not arrestable, they have a lesser part to play, forgetting perhaps about the many other essential roles of the campaign that need to be filled. Everyone is needed in this struggle; everyone is valued; everyone has a vital contribution to make.

Clinging to the truth of the science and trying to face it full on is, paradoxically, much more likely to help us with the anxiety and depression which threaten to overwhelm us than denial. The fact that "the truth will set us free" is never more pertinent than when dealing with our feelings about the climate. Facing the truth enables us to make decisions that will help us take action, and action releases energy which in turn helps us face negative feelings.

Therapist Rosemary Randall, with fellow CPA executive member Paul Hoggett, has researched how climate change activists become politicised: from epiphany, when the person realises the terrifying reality of climate change, through "immersion," when they plunge into researching the facts and talking to others with shared concerns, and then action at whatever level is possible for them.

"With climate change, the anxiety comes from feeling there is nothing you can do. You are at that point when the fight or flight mechanism kicks in, and if you can't act on your fear, it provokes huge anxiety. Action brings relief and also an outlet for the anger," they write.* The active phase may then lead to burnout, but, ideally, people will work through this to arrive at a state of "more sustainable activism."**11**

Greta Thunberg's profound comment that *action leads to hope* can be translated into ways of enabling children to take the initiative, too. In 2018 Greta's demonstration sparked a wave of school strikes,

---

* She also highlighted the latent effects of the denial phase. "A lot of people who are coming into climate action and politics are emerging from states of disavowal, and what characterises that position is that, for good, defensive reasons, you have tricked yourself into thinking there is nothing that needs to be done," adds therapist Rosemary Randall. "With that realisation comes huge shame and guilt and coming through that [into action] is extremely painful." (**15**)

Fridays for the Future, which created a wealth of possibilities for children both to learn about what is happening and to feel empowered in the face of this knowledge. They also had the power to bring the crisis into the news and into the conversation of those previously untouched by the significance of climate change.

Similarly, regular gatherings organised by XR for regeneration enable people of all ages to express their feelings in a safe and accepting environment, and to join with others who are on the same journey of discovery, bound by the same desire to do all that they possibly can to at least try to slow down the impending catastrophe.

Such gatherings build solidarity and help overcome pessimism and inertia, helping to empower us and make possible a hope that rests on realism, not denial. Solidarity with others also builds faith in the future, expressed recently by Josh, a young activist remanded in prison for many months as he awaited trial.

> Faith holds more power than hope, if you're going to be a participant, rather than an observer. Faith is the unshakable belief in something without evidence. You need to have faith that we are going to change the world and that you are going to be a driving force in that transformation. You need to have faith that everything you need and everything you need to know will be provided in the right time and sequence. Even though you can't see the way right now, have faith that the way will be shown to you.[12]

Standing firm in this situation is demanding—intellectually, emotionally and spiritually. It requires a moral strength and endurance, and an ability to continue the struggle long-term, whatever it takes and whatever the cost; an ability to ride the waves of unpopularity and misunderstanding, and commit oneself to what is required for the long haul. We have to resist being thrown off course by the specious arguments of those who are trying to preserve *business as usual* and protect the status quo. As one researcher and lecturer in climate change commented: "We cannot give up; we simply don't have the right."[13]

## ANDY ROSS

*CCA member Andy Ross was arrested during the October 2019 Rebellion in London and charged with obstructing the highway. He was tried on 24th March 2021. Below is his statement to the court:*

I have an MSc in Sustainable Food and Natural resources and my job is assessing the transition of companies to a low-carbon world. As such I have a front row seat in witnessing the inaction which characterises humanity's response to the unfolding disaster of climate and ecological breakdown. I am here because I wilfully obstructed the free passage along Millbank.

I am a conscientious protector of the earth. On 7th October 2019 I wedged myself into the corner of a small wooden box in the middle of the road. No ordinary wooden box but part of an Ark. An Ark—"something that affords protection and safety." No protection and safety that day. An Ark—symbolic of life being preserved through catastrophe. An Ark—a place of refuge on the ever-rising seas. An Ark—something like the incredible planet we live on. We live on an Ark and I wedged myself into that small wooden box to try and save that same wonderful, life-sustaining planet that we all rely on for almost every need. What person of faith, of spirit, of love, would voluntarily leave such a powerful symbol of everything that the earth is and everything we stand to lose if we do not protect it?

I was on Millbank with Extinction Rebellion and Christian Climate Action. The name Extinction Rebellion says it all. Extinction is happening now, every day, everywhere. And we're rebelling to try and stop it. Extinction is final and irrevocable. Once they're gone they're not coming back. This is an existential crisis for many species.

I rebel to speak up for those with no voice, such as coral reefs and fish. These reefs, a unique and wonderful habitat, will die soon. Our laws do not adequately protect them, these voiceless ones, and so some of us are compelled to break those laws for the overlooked to be heard.

Mine was not the criminal act. The criminal acts are the cars which drive over that spot on Millbank all day, every day; the politicians who sit inactive and complicit metres from that spot every day; the corporations headquartered in London that put money before life every day.

History is understood backwards and will vindicate those of us who broke small, insignificant laws in pursuit of real justice, obeying higher laws. If the state choses to find me guilty, know that I was standing with those the state does not recognise, does not protect, does not care about and does not consider.

Biologist EO Wilson talks of the Eremocene—the Age of Loneliness—the age which we are entering. That is why I obstructed a road for a few short minutes. Because the thought of condemning my own children and future generations to the Age of Loneliness due to the inactivity of my generation is too much to bear.

*Faith is a political matter, inevitably.*
Daniel Berrigan

*Jesus—I come before you with empty hands...*
St. Thérèse of Lisieux

*THREE*

# FOLLOWING JESUS

In living out our Christian faith in this time of climate crisis, the greatest help comes to us from understanding ever more deeply the life and ministry of Jesus, and by allowing His Spirit to enter into and live in us, so that He begins to direct all that we must do. Jesus is our model; so we need to study the Scriptures to get to know Him better and we need to sit close to God in prayer to be transformed.

We follow the "gentle revolutionary," Jesus, who in the words of activist John Dear, "confronted every facet of violence with a transforming spirit of nonviolent love." In following Him, we become part of "a people who practice, proclaim and promote God's way of nonviolent justice and love for all."[1] Jesus is our model of love and of life. He was radically obedient to the Father; wholly committed to justice; frequently disobedient to the authorities and unswervingly nonviolent towards all whom He encountered. Jesus is our model for all that we are being called to do.

Jesus, Word of the Father, was born as a human being around 4BC: of a Mother who sang *Magnificat* whilst He lay in her womb. We may forget how revolutionary Mary's Song was; in fact, it was banned in Church services during the apartheid regime in South Africa!

After learning she was pregnant, Mary went to visit her older relative Elizabeth, who lived in the village of Ein Cerim in the Judean hill country. As they greeted one another, the child that Elizabeth was carrying leaped in her womb, in recognition of the Christ before him, for whom, as the uncompromising prophet of the desert, he was destined to prepare. Thus, two of Jesus's early *in utero* experiences were a Prophet's greeting and a Mother's Song. It seems that Jesus had a good start in life—with some of the family at least likely to encourage the prophetic vocation given to Him by His Father!

In his spellbinding study, *Jesus: An Historical Approximation*, Jose Pagola helps us understand the society into which Jesus was born and sets His ministry in context.[2] Jesus was born a Palestinian Jew of parents descended from the family of David. When he was a young child, His parents became refugees in Egypt. When the family returned to Palestine, they went to live in Nazareth, a village of between 200 and 400 people in the northern area of Galilee. Like the rest of Palestine, it was under a brutal Roman occupation which produced all the difficulties and complications for its citizens that occupations do.

Jesus lived with His parents, Mary and Joseph and His brothers and sisters (at least four brothers and several sisters, according to Matthew 13:55-56). He no doubt helped out with His younger siblings when time allowed and would have been well acquainted with the ways of young children. Jesus' family was poor, but not amongst the poorest. Joseph was probably a stone mason or builder rather than a carpenter and he would have found plenty of work in the up and coming town of Sepphoris, a short distance from Nazareth.

Sepphoris had been sacked by the Romans when Jesus was about 3 or 4 years old, and brutal punishments had been handed out in response to a rebellion led by one Simon. This event, so close to Nazareth, must have terrified Jesus' family and all their neighbours, and no doubt was talked about in the family whilst Jesus was growing up. Jesus was clearly His own person at an early age; as we know, when He was 12 years old on pilgrimage to Jerusalem, He broke free from the others and went to the Temple to ask questions of the Jewish rabbis about the Scriptures He had been reading.

Tradition has it that he began his active mission and ministry at about the age of 30 whilst he still lived in Nazareth, presumably at home. He went regularly to the synagogue on the Sabbath and according to the Gospel of Luke (4:18-19), began his mission by reading from the scroll of Isaiah, chapter 61 and claiming to be its fulfilment. This event caused His expulsion from Nazareth; He was lucky to get away with his life, so angry were his fellow worshippers. At some point after that, Jesus made his home in the much larger town of Capernaum—perhaps moving in with Peter and his family.

Jesus was steeped in the Scriptures and frequently quoted from them. He would have immersed Himself in the writings of the Prophets, who insistently called for justice for God's people; in the Wisdom literature and the Psalms, as well as the history of His people and God's gracious dealings with them.

He would have been thoroughly familiar with the many stories of nonviolent resistance to the oppressive regimes under which the Jewish people suffered: the story of the Hebrew midwives (Exodus 2) defying Pharaoh's edict to kill all the Hebrew baby boys at birth; the story of the mother and her seven sons defying the King's order to eat pork and the terrible punishments wreaked upon them (2 Maccabees); the story of Shadrach, Meshach and Abednego's faith in God to save them from the effects of the fiery furnace and of Daniel from the lion's den (Daniel).

He would have read about Daniel's resistance to the King's demand for worship, and of the peaceful, nonviolent but steadfast civil disobedience that Daniel enacted by continuing to pray to God beside his open window, for all to see. Jesus would have read about Queen Esther's courage in speaking to the King on behalf of her people uninvited, risking by this disobedience the outpouring of his wrath. There was certainly no shortage of material in Jesus' religious tradition to help form His own commitment to justice, nonviolence and truth, or His practice of nonviolent resistance intended to bring in the reign of God.

## THE THIRD WAY OF RESISTING EVIL

CCA member David Jenkins, in his challenging little book on the rebel Jesus, points out that Jesus would have been looking at the familiar texts through a different lens:

> In the assembly, Jesus is the dissident voice. He reads the same Scriptures as the leader but his reading subverts the status quo. Whilst the Pharisees routinely emphasised the purity code, Jesus would have been highlighting what the text showed about the mercy and justice of God—a counter-cultural view of God's priorities, His "option for the poor." He says, in essence, "you quibble at the way I read minor laws, whilst you are in gross violation of the Ten Commandments." This Jesus is not so meek and mild. He is a rebel, standing in the line of the prophets of old. And in the process he is making an appeal to the listening poor of the land to make common cause with his movement.[3]

For the compassionate heart of Jesus, the injustice He saw everywhere around Him demanded a response. The injustices of the Roman occupation and the structures of Jewish society both meant that God's gift to His people—the land—had been abused by greed, by those who had rendered many of the poor landless, and at the mercy of the rich. Responding to these injustices was Jesus' primary means of opening God's reign of love to those who were suffering, the poor and the severely disadvantaged.

Others before Jesus had tried to stand up for the poor, and had tried to take on the government of the day by violent rebellion. They had been met with brutal reprisals. Jesus had no wish to lead others into the same fate, nor encounter the total failure of His mission prematurely. His approach showed how evil can be actively and energetically confronted without using force; how it must be resisted, and neither accepted nor appeased nor overthrown with violence.

Jesus found a way to do this, and to engage in nonviolent resistance to the injustices of His day without ever abandoning the ethic of love.

In first-century Palestine, civil and religious authority served and reinforced each other; the religious authorities took part in the collection of taxes paid to the Roman empire. The leaders of the two main religious parties were rewarded by the Romans with wealth and status; they were very unlikely to critique, let alone confront, their Roman masters. As is usually the case under occupation, the indigenous leaders of the people became complicit with their oppressors; "they depended utterly on Rome's good favour for political survival," as theologian Ched Myers puts it, and "made every effort to assure [Rome] that they could and would control their own people."[4]

This is the framework within which Jesus was operating when He actively opposed and disobeyed the law. His disobedience was often to the religious law, but because of the intertwining of the two, His disobedience was equally a threat to the State. It is no wonder that trouble makers like Jesus could only be viewed with suspicion and alarm by both the ruling religious and secular authorities.

Jesus would have perceived how complicit the Jewish authorities were with the oppressive Roman occupier; how corrupt and self-serving they had become and how far away they were from being able to protect their people, let alone the very poor, from their brutal, occupying masters. We can see that, for Jesus, the whole edifice of injustice had to be tackled by confronting it head on, whether within the religious or secular arena.

Jesus begins His public ministry, according to Luke, in the Nazareth synagogue when He reads a redacted version of Isaiah 61. Significantly, He leaves out the words which refer to God's coming in vengeance, and He follows the reading with two examples of God's justice which will inaugurate the Kingdom of God: examples of God's grace offered to "outsiders"—the widow from Zarephath in the territory of Sidon, and Naaman the Syrian. We are told that "when the people in the Synagogue heard this, they were filled with anger." People who have long valued their privileged insider status, do not take kindly to the inclusion of others and the concept of *their* right to justice too.

In short, Jesus began His public ministry by disobeying the religious and cultural acceptance of special status for Israel, and asserting his highly counter-cultural vision of God's inclusive reign of justice and peace for everyone.

After calling His disciples to follow Him, Jesus' first action with them is an illegal one. According to Mark (2:23-24), the group walked through the cornfields and plucked the ears of corn. They were hungry, and the raw grains of corn were good to eat. When confronted, Jesus reminds his challengers of the way David and his men, also hungry, had eaten the sacred bread in the Temple reserved for the priest. Jesus is doing more than simply stealing a few ears of corn and doing so on the Sabbath—both illegal acts; He is also confronting the injustice of poverty and wealth. Myers comments:

> Jesus is going on the offensive... challenging the ideological control and manipulation of the redistributive economy by a minority whose elite status is only aggrandised. Mark constantly argues that solidarity with the poor also means addressing oppressive structures. This may well mean breaking the law."[5]

Jesus is, above all, concerned for those who are at the bottom of the social and economic pile. As well as healing, teaching, caring for them, eating and spending time with them, he wants to help them resist their persecutors. Neither submission nor revolt are helpful responses, but there is a third way: a way that Walter Wink calls vigorous and assertive nonviolence.[6] It is a way which Jesus commends.

## *Turning the other cheek*

"You have heard that it was said 'an eye for an eye and a tooth for a tooth'. But I say to you, do not resist an evil doer. But if anyone strikes you on the right cheek, turn the other also; and if anyone wants to sue you and take your coat, give your cloak as well; and if anyone forces you to go one mile, go also the second mile" (Matt 5:38-41).

Jesus is not telling his listeners to avoid *resisting evil*—which is at the heart of all that Jesus did and was—but He *is* telling his hearers *not to resist evil with violence or act violently* against those who are evil. Neither passivity nor violence are helpful to them in the dire circumstances in which they are forced to live.The first gets them nowhere, and the second is very likely to get them executed. But it is, nevertheless, very possible, profitable and necessary for them to resist. Jesus shows them how.

To be struck on the right cheek was a gesture of humiliation; to turn the other cheek is to reject the intended humiliation—to say 'you failed'—causing confusion for the assailant. The same occurs in our affable and kindly responses to the police, or in the courts when we are arrested. We are asserting our control, paradoxically, over a situation over which we have no control. We, like those to whom Jesus was speaking, are asserting our equal humanity, which is a powerful and effective action against the system of oppression which is trying to dehumanise us.

## *Giving your undergarment*

Jesus also addressed indebtedness. The scene is a courtroom. Indebtedness was an ubiquitous experience for the majority of the Palestinian population, weighed down as they were by the corrupt determination of tax collectors to seize every ounce of revenue from them. When all their land had been taken and the poor could not pay what they were told they owed, it frequently led to court appearances. The very poor might have only the cloak they stood up in to offer in payment—apart from their undergarment. Since nakedness was taboo and its shame fell on the one who was causing it, Jesus suggests that, by offering his undergarment too, and thus ending up naked, the whole system of so-called "justice" is rendered a laughing stock by the person accused![*]

## *Carrying a backpack*

Another of Jesus' examples refers to the practice whereby Roman soldiers stationed in Galilee could require someone to carry their heavy backpack for them—but for one mile only. To require a further mile would attract severe penalties.[†]Thus, Jesus' advice is to offer to do what will undoubtedly cause difficulties and confusion for their oppressors and allow the Galilean peasant to regain the initiative, even in his position of extreme humiliation and powerlessness.[‡] All of these acts can be seen as creative responses to oppression and control, posing dilemmas for the oppressor and compelling him to see the humanity of those who he is oppressing.

## *The disobedience of healing*

Jesus' healing ministry is a study in nonviolent disobedience. It almost seems that He went out of His way to use this ministry to confront the deeper problems of injustice and corruption that lay at the heart of society. "Are there not six days on which you could heal the sick?" the Jewish authorities ask plaintively and reasonably. Yes—surely it was confrontational in the extreme for Jesus to repeatedly choose the Sabbath, when all work was disallowed, to perform so many of His healing miracles! But at each point, Jesus uses the

—

* Shades here of the naked protests that have been held in the UK Parliament and elsewhere to draw attention to the evil of the fossil fuel industry, just as God called Isaiah to go naked for three years to warn of God's judgement on Egypt, in Isaiah 20.

† The point being that Rome tried to avoid giving cause for insurrection if at all possible.

‡ A variation on Jesus' suggestion was taken up by CCA member Bill White during 2022, when he sent double the fine that had been asked of him—a disruptive action indeed in terms of the difficulties that would be caused to the court's accounting system!

occasion for a wider purpose, which is invariably to challenge the rules and laws that keep the people sick. It is society that is sick, and it is not possible to be well within a system that is itself so sick and corrupt. "By making others whole and doing so publicly," John Dear writes, "Jesus denounces the religious culture's inability to heal the poor and broken."[7]

Sometimes too, Jesus flouts other norms and rules, as when He healed lepers and touched them in the process. His touching was a symbol of His inclusive love for them; a healing moment in itself, but deeply contrary to the norms of society, as were the many occasions when He sat down to dinner with the outcasts of society.

Part of the reason this made the scribes and Pharisees so angry was, no doubt, because it showed up their own excluding and rejecting behaviour to those who they deemed to be completely outside their sphere of interest. Prostitutes, tax collectors, the very poor, widows and women generally, were all attracted to this Man who seemed to show no special favours to anyone, and who exuded loving acceptance to all.

Eating a meal with such people, thus demonstrating a special intimacy with them, severely transgressed the accepted rules of society. In Mark 3:34, Jesus also makes the extraordinary statement that all the poor people sitting around Him "were His Mother, His sisters and His brothers." In a society where blood ties called for the highest regard, that was some statement and probably did not endear Him to His family at all!

Jesus was not always nice to people; instead He loved them with an uncompromising love. He was able to love like this because He knew that He was deeply loved Himself. He spent long hours in communion with His Father, aligning Himself with His Father's will, but also experiencing ever more deeply His Father's overwhelming Love. Jesus is God, but His human nature needed to grow in the knowledge of God's love for Him and to experience the meaning and purpose of that love as it flowed out from Him to others.

No doubt Jesus was able to grow in courage, fearlessness and clarity of vision through His deep immersion in His Father's being. His bias towards the poor and His resolute espousal of nonviolence in every situation came from the same source. This last characteristic must have been very frustrating for the many revolutionary groups within Palestine at the time, who felt the need to hasten the overthrow of the Roman yoke by violence. Maybe that was why the people chose Barabbas rather than Jesus when given the choice of which prisoner to set free at Passover. Jesus' way was just too slow and indirect—the people wanted action now.

Jesus easily drew large crowds to listen to Him, but he was often not popular. His uncompromising message; his adherence to the truth; his passion for justice for the least in society—all of this easily made him enemies amongst the rich and powerful.

Jesus' illegal activity is well illustrated by His preparedness to engage with and befriend the enemy. The enemy at the time was both the foreign peoples by which Palestine was surrounded: the Greeks, the Samaritans and the Gerasenes, but also the occupying Roman soldiers and other Roman officials. It goes without saying that fraternising with either group was completely unacceptable, and may have been, in the case of the Romans, illegal and probably treasonable.

But Jesus had come to propose another way of being: a way of inclusive love. So we find Him responding with love and compassion to the request of the centurion for the healing of his servant. We find Jesus frequently travelling to the other side of the lake where the Gerasenes were to be found and, on one notable occasion, healing the man possessed by demons. We find Jesus going into Samaritan territory and having a prolonged theological discussion with a Samaritan woman about the differences between the Jewish and Samaritan religions.

The healing of the Gerasene demoniac also exposes the disruptive nature of many of Jesus' interventions. The sick man was possessed by a load of evil spirits and when asked His name by Jesus, He replied "legion."* Jesus dispatches the evil spirits into a nearby herd of pigs, resulting in an outcry from the owners and onlookers alike. Unsurprisingly, Jesus is requested to leave the area and not come back! The price of healing the possessed man, the price of changing the social order around him and having his life disrupted and transformed is too high and therefore unacceptable.

Civil disobedience can indeed be disruptive; quite often it has to be, if it is to bring about the change that is hoped for and required. All the examples of Jesus' ministry described so far would have caused some considerable disruption in the understanding of the people, because they were challenging the status quo and the way things were done in an unequal and unjust society. But the clearest example of Jesus' disruptive disobedience is, of course, His activity in the Temple, shortly before his arrest—in fact a major factor in bringing his arrest about. Jesus entered Jerusalem in triumph on the back of a donkey, a huge political statement in itself—contrasting His humble Kingship with the oppressive Roman system of governance. He then visited the Temple to look around it and presumably get the measure of the problem.

The following day, Jesus went to the Temple and, taking a whip of knotted cords, proceeded to drive out the money changers and the merchants and all the animals that they were there to sell.

> He overturned the tables of the money changers and the stools of those who sold pigeons and He would not let anyone carry anything through the Temple courtyards. He then taught the people, "It is written in the Scriptures that God said—*My*

—

* It is a clear reference to the Roman occupation, bringing the personal and the political together, the need for the system of oppression to be changed and abolished and the need for the individual who has been so damaged by it to be healed. Jesus is confronted by the complexities of bringing about social and political change and proceeds, as one always must, on both tracks at once but His intervention inevitably causes disruption to those who believe themselves to be uninvolved in the problem.

> *Temple will be called a House of Prayer for the people of all nations*—but you have turned it into a hideout for thieves." *(Mark 11:15)*

It was a disruptive action indeed. Jesus is confronting, head on, the way that the Temple has become wholly intertwined with the secular state, acting as a means of tax collection and sheltering the many officials who are abusing their power. Jesus exposes the financial system behind the injustices that are perpetrated every day on the poorest of the poor. By forbidding people to carry goods through the Temple, Jesus succeeded in shutting down its operations, if only for a short time. We may compare His action with those who "shut down" for a short time the many symbols of destruction that exist in our world today, drawing attention to the need to change our whole way of life as we face the climate crisis. As in the Temple, "business as usual" cannot continue if people, especially the poor, are to live and to thrive. Jesus' action would not have been popular, or indeed even understood, but it was a necessary symbol of the change that had to happen if God's Kingdom of justice and peace was to be inaugurated.

Luke 23:2 records that Jesus was explicitly charged with inciting people to refuse to pay their taxes—an action that would obviously have been seen as sedition, and would have incurred the heaviest of penalties. After his action in the Temple, the Gospel writers record a highly significant interchange between Jesus and the Pharisees. They set him a trick question and it is all about taxes.

> "Tell us, is it against our Law to pay taxes to the Roman Emperor? Should we pay them or not?" But Jesus saw through their trick and answered "Why are you trying to trap me? Bring a silver coin and let me see it."
> They brought Him one and he asked: "Whose face and name are these?"
> "The Emperor's," they answered. So, Jesus said, "Well then,

pay the Emperor what belongs to the Emperor, and pay God what belongs to God."
*Mark, 12:14-17*

It did not take much to see that, since everything belongs to God, there will be nothing left to pay the Emperor if one is being truly obedient to the demands of God's reign. Jesus is teaching that obedience to God always comes first before any claims of the State.

*

The writer of the Epistle to the Hebrews tells us to "keep our eyes fixed on Jesus" (Heb 12:2). He is our model in all that we do. In the Gospel accounts of His ministry, we see Jesus' actions as a response to His obedience to his Father, so that whilst His actions often lead Him into disobedience to the civil and religious authorities, it is *obedience* not *disobedience* that lies at the core of everything He does. Jesus is intent upon revealing the truth of God, and the reality of the way life is, and the way it should be lived. He is concerned, at all times, to reveal to His hearers God's purposes for their lives and the character of God Himself—which is Love, expressed through justice and truth. This is the prophetic nature of Jesus. We are called to follow Him in expressing in and to the world, His truth, His justice and His love.

Jesus' obedience to God was not easy and nor is it easy for His followers; It is costly and demands sacrifice. For Jesus, this led Him to Calvary. His followers are called to follow Jesus on the way of the cross, and Jesus makes it clear repeatedly during His exchanges with those who are considering answering His call, that to follow Jesus demands everything. We are promised little in return in this life other than persecution, misunderstanding and rejection.

In the Sermon on the Mount, Jesus spelt this out:

"Happy are you when people insult you and persecute you and tell all kinds of evil lies against you because you are my followers... This is how the prophets who lived before you were persecuted" (Matthew

5:11-12). But, for those who persevere to the end, this way of truth and love brings the eternal life that is God's ultimate promise and is God's desire for all His children.

The Church finds it difficult, however, to fully embrace the radical nature of Jesus—His behaviour and His teaching—and hard therefore to make His teaching useful and applicable to the dire situation in which we find ourselves. But many Christians *are* now understanding that Jesus calls us out of our comfort zones, into the heart of our current predicament—whatever it takes, whatever the cost.

He is calling us to witness to the reign of God within the climate crisis, and to do all in our power, through nonviolent, unwavering resistance, to overthrow the powers and principalities of evil and bring in His Kingdom of justice and peace. In all that He did and said, Jesus was bearing witness to the character of God. He was showing people the way God was: a God of justice, mercy and peace who desires abundant life and well-being for all His creatures, human and non-human alike.

The God who we worship is the God we see in Jesus, full of pity and love, full of zeal and commitment and intent upon bringing abundant life to all. This is the God to whom we are called to witness *now* by standing against the evils of inertia, false choice, short term gain, cowardice and greed. This is our calling *now*, today: to give the lead, to be a prophetic voice against the principalities and powers of the world, intent upon the destruction of all that God has made.

## SAM WAKELING

*CCA member Sam Wakeling, a father of two young children, was one of seven Christians arrested whilst taking part in a prayer vigil outside London City Airport as part of an Extinction Rebellion protest in October 2019. He was convicted for failing to provide his name and address when asked by a police officer prior to being arrested, despite explaining to the court that he was silent because he was at prayer. Below is his statement to the court.*

I'm charged with staying silent. And for that I am surely guilty. Like so many of us, I have stayed for too long as a bystander. A silent witness of unspeakable things. But the day in question, sitting in prayer at an airport, is the first time my silence has been called criminal.

My crime? Breaking the law is not my intention, and we claim that this country protects in law the right to protest, and the right to practice one's faith. My legal claim is very simple—that according to articles 9 and 11 of the European Convention of Human Rights I was participating in both legitimate protest and practice of well-recognised faith, and that the police's actions in preventing this were not proportionate or necessary, and therefore were not lawful.

I was not the one breaking the law that day. The prosecution has not shown evidence of any threat I was posing to national security, public safety, health or morals, or the rights and freedoms of other people, nor was my presence any cause of disorder or crime. In this upside down world is it not the government of this country who, by gratuitous negligence of failing to respond properly to the climate emergency, are guilty of each and every one of those things?

So I appeal to the rule of law, as independent and providing protection for every person regardless of status? But when the Supreme Court, our highest court, rules as on the Heathrow expansion, that the Paris Agreement should be disregarded rather than holding our government to its own laws, it becomes all the clearer that my faith cannot lie simply in the courts to uphold justice.

I hope instead to speak of where I find and place my faith. Not in the crown but the cross. I have today sworn to tell the truth, and since I am charged with failing to answer why I was sitting on the pavement outside London City Airport, I will give my reasons.

I think back to the day London City Airport opened, on October 26, 1987. 6000 miles away in Cape Town, I am aged three and walking with my mother alongside a busy road on my way to the church playgroup. I wasn't aware of it then, but we were participating in an activity which the South African government then called illegal. The church was multiracial and as such it and its activities were against the law.

It should have been an early clue to me that what a government tries to stop, and even makes illegal, may not necessarily be wrong. And the harder a government tries to silence dissent, the harder we must all look at what they're afraid of people saying.

We are told the UK are world leaders, that innovation will save us, and that everything is somehow under control. Instead of trying to wake us up, those with power seem intent on pressing snooze for as long as they can—moving now from blunt, old-fashioned denial, to instead pointing at distant targets and greenwash, something Prof Kevin Anderson calls "mitigation denial". The result is to further brutalise and steal from people and lands across the majority world in a desperate attempt to prop up this sick and tired world order.

As the prophet Jeremiah said "They dress the wound of my people as though it were not serious. 'Peace, peace,' they say, when there is no peace." Jer 8:10-11

Yet there are many who need no waking up. Millions who have lived with their house on fire for hundreds of years. People who have been on the sharp end of Global Britain. Black and brown people treated as less than human, their lands treated as resources and their labour taken without choice or charge.

For centuries wealthy white men have looked around the world for more of 'nature' to claim as their own and turn into what they can recognise as wealth. This climate crisis does not spring out of thin air, but out of patterns of exploitation, many of which trace back to the City of London. And the City of London, while financing the emissions doing violence to our climate, are also a main customer base for London City Airport.

This airport serves the richest passengers of any major airport in the UK, perhaps the world, with the average incomes of their 5 million passengers in 2019 at around £89k—very literally an airport for the 1%. Aviation kills, yet the vast majority of the world have little or nothing to do with it. Half of all the emissions from passenger air travel globally are caused by just 1% of the world's population. And it is growing. The UK likes to celebrate that since 1990 our territorial emissions have halved. Yet in that same time, and not counted in the territorial figures, emissions from aviation have more than doubled.

London City Airport is determined to continue this growth, especially expanding their capacity for hosting private jets. Months after our actions they announced the airport was now carbon neutral (through buying offsets, and not counting the 95% of their emissions from flights). In 2020 they boasted that while building their new taxiway they saved 3000 tonnes of $CO_2$. They didn't mention that unfortunately this much is then emitted by the flights the airport normally hosts in just the three days you'd need for a long weekend to Amsterdam.

I am afraid, and I do fear for my children—how could I not? They are 4 and 2, and ought to expect to live to see the 22nd century, whatever that might look like. But by no virtue of mine they are some of the safest in this world. They are not likely to find themselves trapped the wrong side of a border, starving while others feast, or denied simple treatments for disease. We in the UK, in one of the least vulnerable parts of the world for climate impacts, cannot stay blind to the reality that this future that we fear is already here for many of our brothers and sisters.

Why did this lead to me sitting in prayer? I can simply say that it was where my body needed to be to feel honest. I've grown up in churches, and have recited the Lord's Prayer countless times. But as the small group of us—including grandparents, and a nun—spoke it sitting on that concrete paving it was more real for me than any time behind stained glass. "May Your will be done, on earth as in heaven" reminds us that this God we seek is profoundly invested in this earth we sit on. This faith I was practicing on that pavement is no call to spiritual escape, but for redemption and transformation of our world's real injustices, through our real, bodily lives.

This is Holy Week, when Christians remember Jesus visiting Jerusalem. He went to the temple, and he turned the place upside down. He could not stand the authorities running systems of economic and racial division and exploitation in the name of God. He turned the tables, scattered their money and quoted ancient prophets saying "my house will be a house of prayer for all nations, and you have made it a den of robbers".

To follow this man, is to follow someone willing to disrupt in order to speak the truth, to demand justice alongside oppressed people. Of course, this got him into yet more trouble, and we all know how the week ended, as the brutal violence of the empire tried to silence yet another troublemaker.

This faith means following a man who told a different story with his actions, who challenged corrupt, racist exploitative power, without becoming like them. He taught his followers to pray and dream that God's Kingdom would come here on earth. For freedom for all God's children, especially those who have been pushed down, marginalised, racialised and made less than. He taught of a Kingdom where the last would be made first, and many who are first now would come last.

My prayer on that ground was a protest, maybe like every prayer is—a dream that another world is possible. Maybe that's foolish. Maybe this government calls it criminal. I don't believe that makes it wrong.

It makes it even more necessary. Whether criminal or simply a fool, I am here today, as I was at the airport that day, a broken man, searching for grace. I'm privileged with everything this crooked world can give, but still starving and thirsty for the freedom that none can have unless we all are free. It is never too late to do what is right. And never too soon to start.

You will pass judgement on my actions. I pray, in the words of the motto over the door: "Lord direct us"—that you, and I, and all God's children may be free.

*When neglect of the call means a denial of God, civil disobedience becomes a peremptory duty.*

Mahatma Gandhi

*I am distrustful of spiritual people who are not roused in their bodies on behalf of justice.*

Cole Arthur Riley

*The problem is not disobedience: it is obedience.*

Howard Zinn

*FOUR*

# WHY WE BREAK THE LAW

For some Christians, being faithful disciples at this time will involve breaking the law. But resisting evil or injustice does not, by any means, *always* involve breaking the law. Civil disobedience is one form of civil *resistance*: a non-violent, organised, public display of collective action, with the intention of influencing or changing the political, social, or economic status quo. This can include strikes, demonstrations, sit-ins, die-ins, marches and occupations; or the ordinary means of resistance to a policy available in a democratic society, such as letter writing, leafleting, lobbying and public meetings.

Anyone who calls attention to injustice; who bears witness to the truth of oppressive behaviour and oppressive structures; who acts to try to change injustice—that person is resisting evil. That is the calling of every Christian.

Engaging in the civil resistance we call nonviolent direct action (NVDA) does not necessarily involve breaking the law either. Most of the thousands of people who attend Extinction Rebellion events, or those who belong to Christian Climate Action, are not arrested. The political scientist Gene Sharp itemised 198 ways of taking nonviolent direct action, only a few of which are illegal.[1] Thus, not all NVDA involvement will lead to conflict with the authorities—like joining the Red Rebels of Extinction Rebellion, for example. The aim of NVDA is simply to agitate and disrupt in the least harmful and least violent way that is possible.*

—

* Many activists would accept that this does not preclude 'violence' towards

Resistance is part of what is involved for Christians in keeping our Baptismal vows, and remains a part of our discipleship throughout our lives. Resistance to evil is required of *every* Christian if they are to fulfil their calling to bring in God's Kingdom on Earth. The traditional works of mercy, to which Jesus refers in Matthew 25, are also calls to take direct action; and so we are all called, in varying degrees, to feed the hungry, care for the sick, visit those in prison and find homes for the homeless.

All of this is direct action, even though the term is more usually reserved for those taking political action to try to change the *system* that renders the hungry hungry and the homeless homeless. In our present emergency, we are called both to change the system that is enabling the climate crisis to continue, *and* to embrace and help those who are suffering now in the global south—and also all who are suffering psychologically in our own society from the anxiety and fear of climate upheaval.

Sometimes, this leads us into civil *disobedience*, where "people deliberately break a law—nonviolently, believing that the law is immoral or unjust—knowing that they will go to prison as a result," as political scientist Erica Chenoweth puts it.[2] It is intended as a means of creating a crisis, fostering tension, so "that a community that has consistently refused to negotiate is forced to confront the issue." This is how Martin Luther King Jr., in his *Letter from a Birmingham Jail*, wrote about civil disobedience.[3]

When I first joined Christian Climate Action in 2017, I was not new to the idea of civil disobedience. At 18, I signed up to the Peace Pledge Union and quickly found myself swept up into a group that regularly distributed leaflets on a local military base, aimed at trying to dissuade military personnel from continuing in their chosen profession. Needless to say, this was an illegal—possibly treasonous—act, and

---

property—such as hammering on the nose cones of nuclear weapons, burning draft papers during the Vietnam war, or glueing themselves to court room furniture.

keen as I was to pursue the idea, my older and wiser companions felt I was a bit too young to embark on a long prison career at 18! It wasn't in fact until I was in my 40s and at Theological College in the early '80s that I was first arrested. I had joined with the Dominicans from Blackfriars, Oxford and a fellow ordinand, for a service of penitence on Ash Wednesday, which we held on the runway of the Upper Heyford American cruise missile base.

I think we just about completed the liturgy before being arrested by the military police. The event marked the moment when I began to connect my Christian faith with the need for civil disobedience. It was also the moment I appreciated that, in many areas, our government was complicit in the pursuit of evil, rather than being concerned with the pursuit of the common good.

Civil disobedience has a long and honourable history, reaching far back into classical Greek literature; although the genesis of the term in its modern form is usually attributed to the American writer and philosopher Henry David Thoreau, who wrote a seminal essay on the subject, published in 1849 under the title *On the Duty of Civil Disobedience*.[4] Thoreau makes the crucial point that citizens ought to disobey government policies and laws which violate their own conscience in order to avoid becoming agents of injustice themselves—that is, in order not to be complicit with injustice or evil.*

So the purpose of breaking the law is to draw attention to something that is gravely wrong and which is being supported and upheld by an institution, corporation or government, which has so far not yielded to any other kinds of pressure. It may also be undertaken in order simply to avoid being complicit in an unjust system, which one cannot

---

* According to Erica Chenoweth, "He was disgusted that his fellow northerners appeared indifferent to slavery and racism. Legend has it that essayist and neighbour Ralf Waldo Emerson visited Thoreau during his night in jail and asked Thoreau why he was there—to which Thoreau replied, 'Why are you *not* here?'" (**12**) A good question indeed, and one which every Christian needs to face.

change, but from which one can withdraw one's consent and thus one's collusion.

It is not something to be undertaken lightly; it requires due preparation as well as profound interior reflection. It bears repeating that there is no hierarchy of obedient response to God: no single way of responding is to be counted as better or worthier than any other. God asks different actions from each of His followers.

Dr. Carmody Grey, in a conversation in a Laudato Si' group on April 14th 2023 about finding courage, commented:

> "(T)here's something about the way in which activism [by which she means civil disobedience] has been defined and pigeonholed, that has really not been good for the climate movement in particular: the narrative has presented people who go onto the street as people who are in some kind of radical discontinuity with other kinds of care, or other kinds of responsibility: rather, it's simply what responsibility looks like in a time like this.
>
> Caring sometimes takes the form of feeding the person next door: at other times it looks like trying to stop oil refineries. We human beings are all on the same side. The courage that activists are showing is on behalf of all humanity. It's not adversarial, more an act of solidarity, trying to bring everybody together into a future that's actually possible for everybody.[5]

## SACRIFICE PREDICATED ON LOVE

The moment of "crossing the line" from legal protest into civil disobedience marks a profound shift for those activists who make this transition. It involves a reassessment of one's identity both as a human being and as a Christian; from someone who habitually keeps the law of the land, to someone who has come to be seen as a criminal. Christians need to take seriously our call to *obey* the civil authorities, other than when they are intrinsically evil, promoting evil policies or are in dereliction of their duty of care. The decision to engage in civil disobedience is a serious one, and the default position will actually always be to obey the state.

Yet perhaps the real task for Christians* is to avoid seeing this as a binary choice: obedience, or disobedience. We should not dismiss the existing social order indiscriminately; but neither can we afford to sacrifice renewal in the name of social stability. The South African philosopher Charles Villa-Vicencio writes "there is a dialectic between stability and renewal. The church rightly rejects both tyranny and anarchy and maintain[s] a stubborn and restless hope for something *more*." **6**

So we find Paul, in his letter to the Romans, insisting that Christians should be good citizens, obey the civil law; honour their rulers, pray for them and pay their taxes. Of course they should, and we should do so today as well! Christians have an obligation to obey the law like everyone else. One might even say that Christians have *more* of an obligation to obey the law; they have a moral duty to do so, because God has provided systems of law in all societies to protect human beings and safeguard the social structures of life that enable life to flourish.

Romans 13 is often cited as a rebuttal of civil disobedience, but there are many other factors at work here. In Paul's time, according to the historian Tacitus, there had recently been a tax revolt and this had been put down with enormous ferocity and cruelty. Paul, whilst frequently in breach of the law himself, nevertheless did not want the embryonic churches to become embroiled in struggles which they could not hope to win and which would likely decimate their numbers.

—

* Nichols and McCarty: Scripture "seemingly emphasise[s] both order and freedom simultaneously, both structure and creativity ... the New Testament recognises the sinfulness of humans and points to the limitations of what can be realised in the political sphere while simultaneously remaining grounded in the confidence and hope that there is more than human sinfulness, for there are possibilities for restoration in God." (**13**)

There were more important battles to be had.

In addition, there were groups of Christians who were arguing that, as the second coming of Jesus was imminent, there was no need for them to engage in civil society at all! Paul was wanting to encourage them to *continue* with their civic responsibilities and to see themselves as contributing citizens, normally obedient to the law and supportive of their rulers—even though now bound in obedience to a higher authority and waiting in expectant hope for the coming of Christ. The witness of the early Church makes it clear that Christians need to take seriously our call to obey the civil authorities *other than* when they are intrinsically evil, promoting evil policies or are in dereliction of their duty of care.

As Martin Luther King Jr put it, "in no sense do I advocate evading or defying the law... I submit that an individual who breaks a law that conscience tells him or her is unjust, and who *willingly accepts the penalty* of imprisonment in order to arouse the conscience of the community over its injustice, is in reality expressing *the highest respect for law*." A "just" law, in King's reckoning, is "a human-made code that squares with the moral law or the law of God. An unjust law is a code that is out of harmony with the moral law."[7]

God's people must always stand up for what is right, and against what is evil, even when from time to time this brings them into opposition with the laws of the land. If and when there comes a moment when the civil law contravenes God's law, then God's law must always take precedence. We find multiple examples, both in the Hebrew Scriptures and in the New Testament, of God's people needing to follow the laws of God when they conflict with the laws of the State. In those circumstances they had to engage in acts of civil disobedience.

The Acts of the Apostles, our primary source for understanding the priorities of the Early Church,[8] gives us plenty of material on its own. Born at Pentecost—when the Holy Spirit was bestowed on the Apostles, upon Mary, Jesus' Mother, on His brothers and on the women who had been His close companions—this little band of followers were immediately empowered, and immediately responded.

Facing a crowd gathered from a variety of cultures and language groups, Peter began to unpack the meaning of the events that had transpired in Jerusalem, concerning Jesus' death, resurrection and ongoing mission. Only days before, Peter and the other Apostles had been huddling together in a room with the doors firmly locked "for fear of the Jews." Not long before that, Peter had denied having any knowledge of Jesus, anxious only to save his own skin. Now, we see the apostles responding to the great gift of the Spirit which had made them courageous, articulate and emboldened to speak the truth about Jesus whatever the cost.

They were immediately laughed at and wholly misunderstood. They surely must be drunk. Undeterred, Peter challenged his audience head on: "God had already decided that Jesus would be handed over to you; and you killed Him." This was not likely to endear him to his audience, but Peter was now full of courage, and able to witness to the truth.

As a result, three thousand were added to the tiny group of believers that day and a pattern of life for the new community began to emerge: learning and teaching about Jesus; fellowship; praying and breaking bread together in Eucharistic meals; eating together and sharing their goods in common. They went daily to the Temple to pray and to sing the praises of God.

The story continues; almost immediately, Peter was in trouble with the authorities. A beggar accosted Peter and John outside the Temple, when they were going in to pray. But instead of giving him money, which they did not have, Peter offered him healing—done in the Name of Jesus. The lame man is immediately cured, and becomes the subject of close attention from a curious crowd of onlookers. Peter does not spare them, fearlessly calling them to account for having killed Jesus, and, at the same time proving by this miraculous healing that Jesus is alive again and has risen from the dead.

The officer in charge of the Temple Guard arrives with some Sadducees—furious that the apostles were teaching that the dead rise to life, much contrary to their own belief. Peter and John are arrested and thrown into jail until the next day, when they are brought before the Jewish leaders and teachers of the law. Challenging the apostles' healing of the lame man, they ask: "How did you do this? What power have you got or whose name did you use?"

Again, we are amazed at Peter's courage, clarity and determination as he answers his accusers: "You should know that this man stands here before you completely well through the power of the Name of Jesus Christ of Nazareth—whom you crucified and whom God raised from death." The Jewish authorities respond by a stern command that the apostles must not speak again or teach in the Name of Jesus of Nazareth. To which Peter replies: "You yourselves judge what is right in God's sight—to obey you or to obey God—for we cannot stop speaking of what we have seen and heard" (Acts 4:19-20).

These words announce the choice that the first followers of Jesus and all His subsequent followers must make: when faced with deciding between God's law and the law of the state or any religious group within it, our choice must always be the law of God.

## THE LAST RESORT

Disobedience is not a natural condition for any of us, and for most people it takes considerable effort. Obedience and compliance are our default positions. The philosopher Frédéric Gros retells the famous story that Ivan tells to his brother Alyosha, in Dostoyevsky's novel *The Brothers Karamazov*—where Christ returns, but is shooed away.[9] No-one, it seems, actually wants to live the way of life that Jesus brings; no one wants to give up their acceptance of the way the world works now, or to receive the freedom to choose life over death.

When Christians undertake civil disobedience and break the law, they do so as a matter of last resort—and because they believe that their action has some hope of success. However, the possibility of success is of much less importance than the belief that it is the right, and only, thing to do in the circumstances; and that it is what God is asking of us.

Christians undertake acts of civil disobedience because they believe it is the only way to remain faithful and obedient to God's calling—the calling to bring in God's Kingdom of justice and peace, for all people and all creatures who inhabit the creation God has made. Thus it is not "disobedience" but "obedience" that is at the forefront of the Christian's mind when he or she breaks the law. At the heart of what they do is *sacrifice predicated on love*, because this is at the heart of the Christian faith itself.

In the Anglican Eucharistic liturgy, we say a closing prayer where we offer our souls and bodies "as a living sacrifice," inviting God to use our offering for the building of His Kingdom. We do what we do out of obedience to God, whatever the cost involved, believing that God is calling us into this particular ministry. And "for many people," as Fr John Dear writes from extensive experience, the moment marks "a new beginning, a new commitment to the Gospel of peace, a new solidarity with our suffering sisters and brothers of the world."[10]

I remember experiencing what I have just written very powerfully on Maundy Thursday 2019, the first time that I was arrested for climate protest. Andrew, my arresting officer, was interested, intrigued and baffled. As is customary, he stayed with me the whole time, which included over an hour waiting to be processed at the police station. We talked about his life, about the action, about the climate crisis and about God. It felt like a great opportunity to engage with this stranger about the most important matters that had brought us together. However, this stranger had complete control over me: I had handed myself over to whatever would come next, and this powerlessness and sense of vulnerability—albeit chosen, not imposed—was for me, paradoxically, a moment of great power. It was a renewed offering of myself to God, for His world—whatever would transpire.

For the Christian, this moment of civil disobedience is, as John Dear puts it,

> certainly a mysterious, meaningful event. If we act with predisposed open, loving hearts, then we will experience the grace of God's Spirit working through us. We may not fully understand what is happening but we will sense that God is present...it is undoubtedly an intense experience. One gets the feeling at such moments that one has been created for such an experience, that it may even be a graced highpoint of one's life.[11]

## PAUL KUNERT

*In June 2021, CCA member Paul Kunert was in court, charged with breaching a Section 14 order at a Rebellion on September 3rd 2020. His defence statement explains why he felt compelled to take action.*

We are called to be keepers of the earth. I am called to be a keeper of the earth, of my neighbour, of all living things. As are you. As is every person in this court-room. It is our fundamental calling, our purpose as humans.

I have been seeking to follow the way of Jesus for many years now. I am compelled as a keeper of the earth. I am compelled by the command of Jesus to love my neighbour. I am compelled to act: to stop the threat to life and livelihoods caused by the Government's failure to act to stop climate change. I've worked for 20 years in Africa and seen with my own eyes the precarious lives of those most affected by rising global temperatures; and I've heard from development agencies working all over the world that this is the most pressing problem faced by vulnerable communities. This is real life, a real world problem, affecting real people, right now. There is a direct connection between the impacts of rising temperatures, the action government here is failing to take, and my actions in Parliament Square last September to urge Government to act.

I have taken what action I can to reduce my own carbon footprint. We've installed an air source heat pump and solar panels; stopped flying; we have an electric vehicle; and we eat less meat. The fact is though that these changes alone will make no noticeable difference to rising temperatures. They will not noticeably help my neighbour. No, it is only by calling on government to act, and government taking action, that this crisis can be averted. My actions on 1 September were the only effective option available to me.

I have never been arrested before. I had no desire to be arrested then. But having done all else reasonably within my power, I was compelled—by love of neighbour, of God's creation, of the natural world, by justice, by necessity—to act as I did, in Parliament Square, on the day on which the Climate and Ecological Emergency Bill was introduced to Parliament, in the hope that our Government, sitting just a hundred metres away, might take notice and act.

The prosecution has not successfully demonstrated that my actions were not necessary. In fact, it must surely be obvious to all in this room that my actions were necessary to prevent a far greater harm; and that they were both reasonable and proportionate in the circumstances. I accordingly submit—in the light of all that you have heard—that I am not guilty of the charge alleged.

*Be concerned above everything else with the Kingdom of God and what God requires of you.*

Matthew 6:13

*FIVE*

# PRAYER, DISCERNMENT AND TRAINING

We are helped in responding to God's call by praying Charles de Foucauld's *Prayer of Abandon* or John Wesley's *Act of Commitment*. They beckon us on, into *letting go*, and doing so every minute of each day, so that we can begin to become *"totus Tuus"*—totally Yours, useful and usable by God in even the terrible crisis that we face today. We are privileged indeed to have been chosen to live at this particular moment in history. Although it may not always *feel* like a privilege, in our better moments we may be able to get a glimpse of the honour that God is doing us, in asking us to live out our Christian faith to the fullest at this particular moment in time.

We have great freedom, but also great responsibility: the responsibility of ensuring, so far as we are able, that we really are following Jesus and not some whim of our own, dictated by our own ego. How, then, do we discern the will of God in the matter of civil disobedience? How do we establish whether a particular action is a good one and, more particularly, is it the right action for me to take and at this particular time?

Christian writers on civil disobedience have suggested different qualifications that need to be met; CCA member Melanie Nazareth, a barrister, suggested these four as key:

1. The situation being challenged must be immoral, in conflict with a higher claim.
2. The action must be reasonable—reasonable as framed by the context of the situation and reasonable because

non-disobedient recourse has been exhausted.

3 There is a likelihood of success. This is partly about the balance of harms, but also about defining success which might not be the conventional way of looking at success.
4 The action is not clandestine and there is willingness to accept the penalty.

St. Paul, ever the realist, knew that both discerning and doing the will of God is not easy:

> For I know that nothing good dwells in me, that is, in my flesh. For I have the desire to do what is right, but not the ability to carry it out. For I do not do the good I want, but the evil I do not want is what I keep on doing. Now if I do what I do not want, it is no longer I who do it, but sin that dwells within me. So I find it to be a law that when I want to do right, evil lies close at hand. For I delight in the law of God, in my inner being.
> *Romans 7:18-24*

The book of Proverbs (3:6) answers these questions like this: "Remember the Lord in everything you do and He will show you the right way." Several verses in Psalm 37 hint at the same direction of travel:

> Take delight in the Lord and He shall give you your heart's desire; commit your way to the Lord and put your trust in Him and He will bring it to pass; He shall make your righteousness as clear as the light and your just dealing as the noonday; be still before the Lord and wait patiently for Him
> *Psalm 37:4-7*

In *The Sacrament of Civil Disobedience*, John Dear provides several schema for assessing whether or not engaging in civil disobedience is what God is asking. These are drawn from a variety of sources: Pax Christi; Ploughshares; various US Peace groups; Ignatian Spiritual Exercises; and the Northern Ireland Peace People. They repay careful attention and are to be highly recommended for our individual use and for use within our groups.

In trying to work out what God wants of us in a particular situation, we are invited to become very conscious of God's Presence within us. We are asked to be still before that Presence, to wait upon Him, to trust Him and to let God know that all we want is to do what God wants. In other words, the primary tool for us to use in discerning God's will is prayer. Jesus spent long hours in prayer before all the major decisions of His life, being very close to His Father and listening to the silence of His Word. We need to do the same. We need to sit at God's feet in silent, surrendered prayer and see what happens.

Sometimes what happens is that we emerge from our prayer time full of ideas, full of clarity, full of desire to get on with it, whatever it is. This happens surprisingly often, in fact! But not always. We then need to engage with others in prayerful discussion, "testing the spirits" as St Paul describes it, asking for their help in discerning where sin is creeping in. *Are we being directed by our ego rather than God's will? What's in it for us?* Or, if we are refraining from engaging in civil disobedience, *are we giving way to cowardice? Are we forgetting that God will be with us, giving us the courage we need at the point of our need?*

Other people are more likely to spot where we are being misled in our decision-making by our own emotional needs; they can encourage us or restrain us from action as needs be. Even if we feel sure, after our own time of prayer, that an action is right for us to be part of or not, it's an important exercise to check things out with others before making a commitment. We may not, of course, have to do this in detail before every action, if the action forms part of a holistic response. For example: when a judge recently decided to prevent defendants, on trial in the Crown Court for public nuisance, from telling the jury *why* they had taken the action they did, most of the defendants made a blanket decision that we would disobey this ruling in each of the upcoming trials (see chapter 7).

Otherwise, we may test the appropriateness of an action with a church house group to which we have belonged for years and whose members know us well; or with a core group of CCA with whom we meet for daily prayer; or a Green Christian Way of Life group whose members we know and trust; or a group within XR who meet regularly together. It may also be any number of groups or individuals, whether Christian or not, who have insights into us as individuals; good friends who will tell us truthfully and bluntly what they think of our ideas! An important other resource for us to use in the discernment process may be a spiritual director/soul friend.

Our attentive reading of Scripture will be another resource; maybe using a well-tried method such as *lectio divina*. Some of us will be bound by our clerical promises to pray the daily office twice a day, which will involve at least two and maybe four readings from the Scriptures for us to ponder. Or any Rule of Life will usually include a pattern of daily Bible reading with perhaps notes to help us. God can, and often will, use these set Scripture readings—chosen by Him, rather than us—to reveal what it is He wants us to do. When after prayer, Bible study and discussion with others, clarity does emerge, it is often a moment of great joy.

Ruth Jarman, a founder member of CCA, put it like this in a letter to me just before taking a very high risk action:

> I am sure I should be here. If I was a poet, I would write something about us being arrows—perhaps, green, perhaps orange—flying sharp and free from the bow that is the prayer and love of CCA supporting us—knowing that if we go off course and fall, we will be cushioned by those same prayers. There's something pure and sharp and true about doing these actions—I feel totally liberated.. I have one thing to do. Nothing else matters. And I'm doing it for God, for my children, for all children, for flooded Pakistan, chestnut trees, hedgehogs, you! There is a purity and simplicity about this moment.

People often seem to have their decision to commit acts of civil disobedience confirmed after they have taken the decision and taken part in the action. That in itself is a powerful confirmation that their decision was a true discernment of God's will, and helps them discern how to make further decisions to take action in the future.

Without a clear commitment to being arrested in advance, Jo Rand, a Methodist minister, writes as follows about her experience at the Extinction Rebellion protest in London in 2019:

> I felt a huge sense of peace about what I was doing, about what was happening to me. That surprised me. The process of being on the bridge, of being arrested. I felt completely calm, that I was in the right place, and where God wanted me to be. I've had a real sense that God is calling me to be part of this.[1]

On the same occasion in 2019, another member of the clergy, CCA member Hilary Bond, wrote as follows: "Hours later, I found myself kneeling on the floor of a police cell overflowing with thankfulness and peace; powerfully aware of God's Presence and the knowledge that I was exactly where God wanted me to be. I still have that peace".[2] A laywoman, Sam Lindo commented after her experience in similar vein: "I knew in that moment that this was one of the most meaningful moments of my life. I felt I was exactly where I was meant to be, doing what I was meant to be doing. Acting in nonviolence. Demanding justice. Telling the truth. It felt not only wonderful, it felt divine."[3]

CCA member Fr Martin Newell comments:

> There are certain groups of people who in reality have more freedom to risk going to prison and so to my mind they have more obligation to consider and discern whether they should do this, whether God is calling them to act in this way. Security of home, and of work or income is a factor. Those who are retired and in reasonably good health, for example. Especially those who own their own home without a mortgage. They

> have nothing to lose. Younger adults, who have yet to start a family, and so are without dependents in that way. Clergy, and members of Religious Orders, who have almost total security of job and home. In those cases, if anyone was to challenge you about getting arrested or going to prison, all you have to do is quote the biblical precedents and the life of Jesus. This kind of security is one reason why some people have always looked for life in community, or to build a deeper sense of sharing of economic resources, to enable more people to take such risks.[4]

The same point was made by activist Morgan Trowland, in a blog written soon after he started his three-year prison sentence in 2023: "Disruptive acts must be taken to reduce the harm and loss of the climate and ecological crisis. Who should take those acts, if not the people who will suffer least for taking them?"[5]

Discerning God's will may be as mundane as coming to recognise that one is now too old or disabled to do much else to serve the climate protest movement other than sit on roads and get arrested! A once-clear brain may now find difficulty in following and responding to the arguments of climate deniers; a once-energetic body may not now be able to walk long pilgrimages. But even in old age, most of us can sit on a road or block an oil tanker from delivering its load! The elderly are more usually free of other obligations, too, which might rightly impede the ability of the young. Remembering that God always chooses the weak things of this world to confound those things that are mighty can give those of us who fall into this category the confidence and determination to join with younger friends to do what is needed.

An important part of discernment is to ponder what other contributions one could make, and ought to be making, to the protest movement. It may not be sensible to end up in prison, when the greater need is to do the mundane work of recruiting new supporters, by leafleting and speaking at recruitment meetings. Engaging in civil disobedience and ending up in custody may be a form of escape from the routine tasks of the protest movement or a way of avoiding other obligations at home or at work. The proposal for action always needs scrutinising with these thoughts in mind and laying before the Lord.

Our engagement in acts of civil disobedience in order to address the injustices of climate change is likely to be authentic to the extent that the search for justice and the desire to bring justice to others informs the rest of our Christian life. If we have no interest in the marginalised and dispossessed in our communities—the homeless, those in food and fuel poverty, asylum seekers, the lonely—we might question whether God wants us to roll up our sleeves and engage in some practical service to them before embarking on the more dramatic work of civil disobedience. Likewise, if our own lives are filled with family tension and neighbourly disputes, we may perhaps wonder if God wants us first to work on these areas of conflict and violence in our lives before committing ourselves to the deep nonviolence of civil disobedience.

We need to trust God's promise that the Holy Spirit will lead us into all truth. If, as far as we can know ourselves, our intention is truly to do God's will and to be effective workers for the Kingdom in the sphere of protecting God's people and creatures from the threat of climate catastrophe, we can reasonably believe that His Holy Spirit will lead us along the path that He wants us to tread.

Dear writes as follows:

> Ultimately, an act of nonviolent civil disobedience is an act of divine obedience; that is, it is a response to the movement of God's spirit in our world, encouraging us to stand up and risk a public act of peacemaking on behalf of those who suffer. It is a way to respond publicly, faithfully, and politically to our nonviolent God. Ideally, our engagement in civil disobedience should always come as a response to this movement of God in our lives.[6]

Kittle makes a further important point:

> Thought must always be given to the ethics of specific actions. Due to the nature of civil disobedience and the risk of arrest, each person considering it should be convinced in their mind, not just that it is morally permissible, but that it is appropriate for them in their circumstances. Neither XR nor CCA should demand it of any of their members, for while it is morally permissible, that does not make it morally obligatory.[7]

Our motives for undertaking acts of civil disobedience are likely to be very mixed and we are unlikely to be able to get to the bottom of them all; but the effort to do so is important. For example, we may experience a lot of anger at the way in which God's creation is being destroyed and polluted, and his creatures abused. Anger is a powerful motivating force for action; but it can never be the main motivator for the Christian. Love is our only reason, and it's important for us to test the depth and breadth of our love when considering the call to civil disobedience.

Is our desire in taking action primarily to be obedient to the God of Love, or is it more to do with acting out our desire to destroy the "system", attack the fossil fuel industry, express our hatred of the class structures of society, indulge our long repressed iconoclastic urges by being rude to the police, judges or other court officials? Considering what it truly means to be *nonviolent*—in word and thought as well as in deed—can help us discern our shortcomings in this regard. An inherent part of transforming the world is transforming *ourselves*.[8]

## GETTING TRAINED

CCA is closely linked to XR and, being a much smaller group, it makes sense for us to participate in the wealth of training opportunities and support provided by XR as we prepare to engage in civil disobedience.

The Insulate Britain and Just Stop Oil Campaigns also provide tailor-made training events which are essential for all who will take part in these actions.

In addition, CCA provides a weekly seminar, which is likely to be a theological reflection, or a Biblical exegesis of texts relevant to protest, or a discussion about a particular issue: the difficulties being experienced by minority groups in joining in climate protest; an examination of white supremacy, neo-colonialism and the legacies of empire; the problems of self-harm and how to view sacrifice in a healthy and life-affirming way.

Extinction Rebellion, Insulate Britain and Just Stop Oil provide online training in a huge range of activities relevant to taking and supporting climate protest. XR is divided into regional and affinity groups, and members of CCA tend to join in these groups and may in fact undertake most of their direct action as part of their XR team. Belonging to a support group of some kind is an essential element of taking action; CCA members may belong to a regional CCA group which becomes their support group, with the inclusion of others for actions. There are also special interest groups such as Grandparents for a Safe Earth, XR Elders, XR Scientists; XR Doctors, Youth for Climate Action etc. all also organised into local groups and providing a place to which to belong.

Fundamental to all direct action is training in nonviolence. This training is mandatory and ongoing for all members of XR, CCA and related groups going on actions. Side-by-side with this training are workshops in de-escalation. Every team that takes part in high risk action with JSO or IB will have with them at least two de-escalators, trained to speak with the public and the police and able to lower the emotional temperature when hostility is being shown to the protestors. When the protest involves a major disruption to a motorway or other public place, there is also a well-thought-through "blue light policy" of which all protestors are made aware, so that emergency vehicles and others in special need are not prevented from passing, by protestors being glued to the road.

Since the advent of Insulate Britain and Just Stop Oil—groups that have emerged out of XR, prepared to take more radical direct action and more likely therefore to end in prison sentences—other training events are now provided such as "Building Trust and Courage" and "Preparing for Prison." All groups are encouraged to take part in training for speaking to the press and becoming acquainted with knowing one's legal rights, especially since the passing in the UK of the Police, Crime and Sentencing Act in 2022 and the Public Order Act in 2023. XR, Insulate Britain and Just Stop Oil are supported by specialist legal teams which are connected into law firms that specialise in protest law. The legal teams support protesters as they prepare for trial in the courts. A group of supporters are always present in court when protesters are on trial. Another team supports protesters during the time they are in prison, keeping them connected with family and friends and helping them get items they need while in prison.

All actions are supported by a back-office team, which takes phone calls from protesters in police stations or prison, and can pass news on to the protester's family as well as organise police station support for them when they emerge from custody. This latter may also involve finding accommodation for the protester and taking them to it if the person emerges from the police station in the small hours of the night.

There are many roles to fill, and discernment includes discovering which of these roles we are being called to take on. For high risk action, as undertaken by Insulate Britain and Just Stop Oil, safe houses are provided to accommodate the team before and after the action. For these, a pair of volunteers is needed to provide and cook food, run the house and make sure there is clean bedding for an incoming group. These volunteers are essential members of any action team, providing both practical and emotional support to the team before and after the action.

CCA has become a welcome part of protest action within XR, IB and JSO. This gives us opportunities, from time to time, to talk with our fellow protesters about the faith which drives our motivation for action; many of us have found that they are surprisingly open and eager to talk about faith issues and spiritual matters in a broad way, and sometimes about the Christian faith in particular. More important, perhaps, is the sense that we are able to demonstrate—by our presence—the Church's deep concern about these matters which concern us all. We are sometimes able to articulate and make sense of the sacrifices which we are being called upon to make, because sacrificial love is at the heart of our faith; and despite the demands upon us, we can join with others in joyful solidarity, knowing that we are giving all we have and all we are in a supreme effort to make a difference.

## PREPARING FOR ACTION

Part of our preparation for action, as Christians, is prayer. We often have to start early in the morning; so, if there are several of us, we might be praying aloud as we travel to the action in the van. (We always ask the others if that's OK with them).

I remember, on one occasion, arriving early for the action. Several of us gathered in a woodland and said Morning Prayer together. Others drifted around, some joining in or just sitting and listening. When we finished, one of the non-Christians began to sing—a beautiful, haunting song—her offering to the morning skies making our little act of prayer complete.

When Fr Martin Newell and I took part in an action on top of a DLR train, Martin prepared by writing a litany for us to say together. It was called *A Litany for the Earth*. After we had prayed silently, and talked with people who were on the platform below us, we started to pray the litany:

God, we lament the destruction that has been done
**That we have permitted to be done**
By our silence and inaction
**And by our direct action**
To the Earth—Your creation.
**Forgive us, Oh God.**

Perhaps it was the fact that we were praying in humility for forgiveness for *ourselves*, but the crowd on the platform fell silent; and so we continued praying the Litany for perhaps 10 minutes. When we came to court for trial for this action, the Judge asked for printed copies of the Litany to be given to all the jury members. He seemed to recognise that what we were praying for lay at the heart of the matter.

Sometimes we plan a Eucharist as part of the action, which takes thought and preparation. CCA member Revd Helen Burnett has presided over memorable Eucharists in Parliament Square and Whitehall with fifty or more attending.

As part of the Faith Bridge action in 2019, CCA member Fr Jonnie Parkin presided at a celebration of the Eucharist on Millbank. For some reason, the police had decided to completely block the highway, with a double row of officers watching over a small group of protestors. Jonnie processed the Sacrament through the somewhat bemused ranks of police until he reached those of us still sitting on the road to offer us Communion as we waited for our arrest to take place.

If the action is planned for a Sunday, we obviously make preparations for having a Eucharist in the hope that this will be possible. One early morning, during a Just Stop Oil protest in the Spring of 2022, three of us had taken up residence in front of an oil tanker. It was bitterly cold. Other tankers surrounded us, each with protesters on top, braving the iciness, whilst others glued onto the sides of the tanker, the lethal flow of oil brought to a halt, if only for a short while.

A little white cloth, bread and wine and some vessels to hold them were laid out on a stool which had appeared from nowhere. Birds were singing. The sun was beginning to rise behind the oil tanker: silk threads of turquoise, orange and mauve, marbled into a quickly changing kaleidoscope of colour. I remember hoping someone was taking a picture of this quite beautiful sight.

We wanted to call others to join us, but the police refused. So just the three of us celebrated the Sabbath together. What a complete and unmitigated joy, to enable the Lord to become present in this special way, amidst the death and destruction being prepared all around us by the continuous flow of oil. After receiving Communion, we sat in silence, watched and prayed.

*O Radiant Dawn—penetrating the evil of this place with the mystery of Your Presence, revealing Yourself in bread and wine.*
*O Radiant Dawn—overcoming our complicity in it all by Your acceptance of our sacrifice.*
*O Radiant Dawn—piercing through our darkness and our fear with Your Glory and Your Grace.*

The police allowed us to finish before arresting us. It was a moment of great mystery and power.

*

Things don't always go according to plan, of course. The following week was Palm Sunday, and the beginning of Holy Week. We had arrived outside an oil terminal and sat down at the main gates while some of the group were breaking into the sheds. It happened that several of us sitting there were Christians and this intrigued one of the police who were now surrounding us. We discovered that he was an Eastern Orthodox Christian who would celebrate Holy Week and Easter the following week. He seemed intent on deflecting his fellow Christians from getting arrested during our special holy time, and he began begging us to leave.

He was very persuasive! Clearly it would be a feather in his cap if he succeeded, as we almost never leave a protest site before the arrests occur. It seemed that the consensus was to accede to his request, much encouraged by the offer of a lift to the station in a police van! So the Eucharist was celebrated, instead, in the garden of St. John's Church Waterloo, followed by a grateful return to our safe house and a more comfortable night than in the police cells.

Our faith commitments are a mutual sharing, and one of the beautiful bonuses of becoming part of these actions is the way in which we can participate in creating the diverse community that God has called together—crossing boundaries of age, race, culture, background, sexual identity, education, work experience, religious belief and faith. None of these things matter; we are drawn together to create a new community of mutual care, from which we draw strength and inspiration, and learn so many new and lovely things from it.

We have to rely upon each other in dangerous and frightening situations, and this gives us the support and the courage that we need. The safe houses to which we go to take part in an action and to which we return afterwards (if we have not been arrested) are always full of gentle energy, and often fun. When we get there, we know we have arrived; it is all in God's hands now, as it always has been.

## PRAYER OF ABANDON

*Charles de Foucauld*

*Father, I abandon myself into Your hands.*
*Do with me what You will.*
*Whatever You may do, I thank You.*
*I am ready for all. I accept all.*

*Let only Your will be done in me*
*And in all Your creatures.*
*This only I ask O Lord.*
*Into Your hands I commend my spirit.*
*Father, I offer myself to You with all the love of my heart.*
*For I love You Lord and so need to give myself to You*
*And with boundless confidence*
*To surrender myself into Your hands without reserve.*
*For You are my Father.*

## COVENANT PRAYER

### John Wesley

*I am no longer my own, but thine.*
*Put me to what thou wilt, rank me with whom thou wilt.*
*Put me to doing, put me to suffering.*
*Let me be employed for thee or laid aside for thee, exalted for thee or brought low for thee.*
*Let me be full, let me be empty.*
*Let me have all things, let me have nothing.*
*I freely and heartily yield all things to thy pleasure and disposal.*
*And now, O glorious and blessed God, Father, Son and Holy Spirit,*
*thou art mine, and I am thine. So be it.*
*And the covenant which I have made on earth, let it be ratified in heaven.*
*Amen.*

*We must treat arrest as the normal condition of life of a non-cooperator.*

Mahatma Gandhi

*You will know the truth and the truth will set you free.*

John 8:32

*SIX*

# SPEAKING TRUTH

The moment of arrest signifies the beginning of a process whereby we live out our commitment to civil disobedience, and open up the opportunities afforded by a court appearance to bear witness to our beliefs, in public. In the UK at the time of writing, an arrest by the police is usually preceded by a five-stage warning. Thereafter, various choices as to whether to "go floppy" and be carried off or walk away accompanied by the arresting officer have to be made.

Sometimes, and maybe increasingly, protesters are dragged off the road by police with no warning given—and occasionally, if glued on, ripped off the road as well. Protesters in other countries may fare considerably worse.

Following arrest, the courtroom is the obvious place where climate protest can continue and truthful witness be made. "It is a place," writes John Dear, "where the Spirit can be unleashed to address the evils of systemic injustice and institutionalized violence."[1] As Jesus said himself: "When they lead you away and hand you over, do not worry beforehand about what you are to say. But say whatever will be given to you at that hour. For it will not be you who are speaking but the Holy Spirit" (Mark 13:9-11).*

Since 2018, hundreds of climate crisis resisters in the UK and around the world have been arrested and have given their testimonies

---

* Jesus was taking as read the distinction, later spelled out in the first epistle of Peter and elsewhere, that we are not talking about arrest and trials for criminal offences of violence, theft, financial irregularities, corruption etc, but trials brought about by the state's pushback against those taking a principled stand against evil.

in court as to the truth of climate science and the need to respond in the face of government inaction—I have included some of their testimonies throughout this book.

The early church quickly settled into the understanding that being a Christian in itself would bring one into conflict with the state, and this would have predictable consequences. Part of the Christian's witness then, as now, would be to testify in court as to why one has taken the action that one has, and to use the opportunity afforded by the court to witness to one's beliefs and to the acceptance of their cost.

Where this is still possible and still allowed, the opportunity needs to be grasped with both hands; the trial may still afford the protester a unique opportunity to witness to the truth. We do not therefore accept a "caution" after an arrest in order to avoid a trial unless there are pressing personal circumstances which prevent us from seeing the action through to its end point.

For us, as we protest the inaction of governments in the climate emergency, our witness involves speaking truth to power in the courtroom, in so far as we are still allowed to do so, as to the veracity of the science of climate change and the necessity of taking urgent, immediate, radical action to slow down the impending catastrophe.

In so doing we are also attesting to our Christian faith, because our actions are predicated on our belief that God is the creator of the planet and we are its stewards, not its owners or masters, and we have not been given the right to exploit it. We witness to the fact that in taking the extreme action we have taken in breaking the law, and sounding the alarm to persuade governments to act, we are following the radical prophetic Jesus who is the author and finisher of our faith.

By going on trial and speaking publicly of our beliefs, we are therefore being given the immense privilege of attesting to our faith in a public, secular arena, and demonstrating our faith to all whom we encounter by our respectful, courteous, loving but unwaveringly truthful behaviour.

Winning the case is not our main objective. It may be important to try to win, because in doing so we are helping people to understand the climate crisis and how, in order to persuade governments to change course, some people need to engage in radical acts of civil disobedience. Winning the case is important in terms of witnessing to the truth of the climate emergency; but it should not be of consequence to the individual themself. Being found guilty is part of the sacrifice that is being offered and made.

However, we would normally plead "not guilty" unless there are pressing personal circumstances that prevent us, because that is the truth; it is not we who are guilty, it is the government.*

In the UK it is legal to break one law in order to honour a higher one; for example, it is legal to cause criminal damage by throwing a brick through the window of a burning building in order to rescue a child. Thus, climate activists believe they are acting legally in breaking laws in order to rescue children now and in the future from a burning world. Pleading not guilty usually provides greater opportunities for speaking in court. It is also a clarification of the truth.

## RESISTANCE FROM THE SYSTEM

At Gandhi's famous 1922 trial, he pleaded *guilty* to all the charges: "(T)he only course open to you, the Judge, is... either to resign your post, or inflict on me the severest penalty, if you believe that the system and law you are assisting to administer are good for the people." Although arrested many other times subsequently, he was never allowed to make a statement in court again—his words were too potent![2]

As the struggle intensifies between those protesting against the

—

* A point famously made by Nelson Mandela, during the anti-apartheid trials of eleven members of the ANC in 1963 (and no doubt by many other defendants before and since), when charged with sabotage and conspiracy. "My Lord, it is not I but the government that should be in the dock. I plead not guilty." (**16**)

deepening climate crisis and the governments they are protesting about, the opportunities to witness to the climate crisis in court are increasingly being closed off. Defendants in both Magistrates and Crown Court trials were finding that it was not too difficult to persuade a judge or jury into a "not guilty" verdict by speaking the truth about the climate emergency and demonstrating that the need to highlight the emergency was the motivation for their actions.—the last thing the state was wanting to happen. Thus judges are increasingly ruling—in relation to crimes of public nuisance for example—that there are no legal defences available to defendants and that therefore defendants cannot speak about their motivation

This has led to ruling out any mention of the climate crisis as a motivating factor for the action, together with any mention of one's Christian faith, as these are deemed to be "irrelevant." One is simply being tried on the extent of disruption that has been caused, so that the reasons and motivation for taking the action are all disallowed. Other charges of aggravated trespass and criminal damage to property are being handled in the same way. All of this is a measure of the fear and anxiety of the establishment and highlights the need to engage, if at all possible, the judicial system itself as an ally in the struggle.

This was well illustrated in May 2023 when a member of the campaign was so incensed by the Judge disallowing defendants from speaking about the motivation for their actions that the next day she held up a placard at the Jury entrance to the court saying "Juries are allowed to acquit according to their conscience." She was arrested for contempt of court and referred to the Attorney General. This provoked another 24 members of the campaign into replicating her action, sitting at the Jury entrance outside the Crown Court two days running. The Judge referred all 24 to the Attorney General and we await the outcome!

Notwithstanding the recent introduction of these impediments to speaking the truth, it is nonetheless vitally important that we continue to try to do so. Each defendant will have taken a solemn promise to "Tell the truth, the whole truth and nothing but the truth." So to be told by the Judge immediately afterwards that he or she is not allowed to speak about motivation or about climate change or any related topic is clearly a contradiction and one that must be challenged. Several defendants broke through this embargo during the Spring of 2023, and, after refusing to apologise for their behaviour, were sent to prison for several weeks.

There will be moments in the trial when we can ask leave to question the Judge's decision. He will dismiss the Jury, and one will have the chance to ask for his reasons for excluding the points one wants to make in one's witness statement. One may also want to draw attention to the bias one is perceiving in his guidance to the Jury and in other decisions he is making. It goes without saying that these confrontations need to be done with proper regard for courtesy towards all who are in the courtroom at the time.

Some climate resisters have used the court to register their refusal to comply with the legal system at all. Not turning up for trial; not completing preliminary paperwork or acting in court in such a way that the Judge or Magistrates are not shown respect are all ways of "disobeying in court." For a Christian to do so raises difficulties about how this honours the individuals concerned, even if not the institution he or she represents. It can be done, but it requires careful discernment and preparation.

In the case of Insulate Britain and Just Stop Oil, the campaigns challenged the courts to find defendants not guilty in the face of the enormity of the threat to humankind. The government retaliated, and directed that a civil case should first be brought by National Highways against Insulate Britain defendants, to ensure that draconian penalties could be imposed: enormous court costs, automatic imprisonment and the threat of unlimited distraint of assets.

I was charged with "public nuisance" on four occasions for the actions on motorways. As the Judge's restriction on what we could say became more pronounced, I found myself emboldened by the anger that it stirred in me as well as by the absurdity of the situation: dozens of highly reputable, conscientious citizens being muzzled and prevented from speaking their truth about the impending climate catastrophe; dozens of otherwise law-abiding people viewed as criminals for blocking traffic for a short time whilst the government was freely leading their citizens towards untold suffering, death and disaster and incurring no penalty at all.

In particular, I realised how impossible it was for me to take the oath in court to tell the truth, the whole truth and nothing but the truth and then be forced by the judge to immediately break it. Telling the truth is fundamental to the Christian faith. How could I tell the whole truth to the jury when the Judge forbade me to tell them of my motivation, intention and purpose for taking the action? I needed to explain to the Jury that our extreme and outrageous action could only be understood in relation to our desire to interrupt humanity's mad dash towards climate catastrophe.

I had challenged the judge early on in the proceedings to stop acting as a government stooge, and join instead those lawyers involved in challenging the government's climate change "policies." His reply to me had been: "Do you want me to break my juridical oath?" I quoted this back to him, asking whether he expected *me* to break the solemn oath that I had just taken, to tell the whole truth, on the book that is sacred to me, the Bible. His reply was memorable and it showed up my lack of preparedness and my failure of courage in my inability to answer him. "God's law may operate elsewhere, but in this courtroom it is only my authority that is of importance."

Amazingly, given the judge's restrictions, we were given, on that occasion, a unanimous "not guilty" verdict by the jury. Afterwards, for the press release, I said:

> Despite all the odds, I am thankful that twelve of my fellow
> citizens were able to see the bigger picture and even when

> directed by the judge to find us guilty, they were able to understand that the unprecedented times in which we live call for us all to step out of the box and make courageous decisions. Thank you jury. I think reasonable people can see that inconveniencing a few people on their way to work does not compare with the appalling threat to humanity caused by the blindness, stubbornness and greed of just a few people, including our government. We must keep on doing our best, giving our all and obeying God's calling to us.[3]

As the trials proceeded, we gained confidence and courage, and found ourselves able to answer these challenges. For myself, this did indeed feel like a breakthrough, despite the consequences. And how little the fact of being sent to prison or its equivalent weigh in the balance compared with the certain knowledge of doing what one believes to be the right thing to do—or, in the case of a Christian—what God is asking us to do. How joyful an experience is that!

During the fifth trial of Insulate Britain defendants in February 2023, the Judge's restrictions on speaking out about climate change were fully challenged by one of the defendants, David. Having done so, he refused to apologise to the Judge and was given a custodial sentence of 8 weeks. As he awaited sentence, David said to the Judge:

> I'm at peace with my position, even though there are consequences and I'm now in your hands. You will have to live with this moment in the future; you will have to live with your decisions.
>
> I see what happened this week as a kind of climate action delay. Today, BP announced record-breaking profits, and this is the same day that I'm in court because I'm not allowed to speak about climate change....I broke the court rules, but to highlight what is going on. The judiciary at the moment is not protecting life. I'm trying to uphold the rule of law because, if tipping points are breached and we don't have a stable climate

like the one we've had for 10,000 years, the rule of law won't survive when people are hungry.[4]

At the ninth trial, three defendants came before a jury, again charged with public nuisance. After 12 hours' deliberation, the jury were not able to come to a conclusion. They were dismissed, and the trial ended. As in the previous trial, two of the defendants were charged with contempt because they had disregarded the Judge's rulings and spoken of the climate emergency; they were sentenced to 7 weeks in prison.

Amy, one of those sentenced said during her trial:

"The climate crisis and fuel poverty are killing people now, and I will not be prevented from saying this to a Jury. When our so-called leaders are failing us, ordinary people have to step up. This is my motivation, and it *is* relevant."[5]

Afterwards a KC commented: "It may be time for the ancient defence—Duress of Circumstances—to be updated to meet the current climate crisis and be available for all those citizens who are compelled to protest on behalf of the planet and its survival."[6]

Defendants from those trials that remained began to see that the task now was to do all in their power to persuade the judiciary to move towards seeing the survival of the human race as requiring their support.

## LEARNING FROM OTHERS

For most of us, the whole process of being arrested, detained and going to court is frightening and unwelcome. Daniel Berrigan—a leading peace activist in the 1970s and 80s—was arrested and tried on multiple occasions. His whole life was given to the struggle to oppose the production and threatened use of nuclear weapons, whatever the cost to himself. And even he admits in his testimony, "I wish I hadn't had to do it. That has been true every time I have been arrested, all those years. My stomach turns over. I feel sick. I feel afraid. I don't want to go through this again... the push of conscience is a terrible thing."[7]

Yet the experience of managing to stand up in court, conquer one's fear and speak the truth about the climate crisis, when the government and media are largely withholding this truth from the public, begins to feel very empowering.

Even when, given recent rulings, we cannot so easily speak openly to the jury, we may still be able to interrupt the court proceedings by demanding space to explore these matters with the judge and prosecution. We are still being given a unique opportunity—a public platform with the media present, an opportunity not to be missed. Gradually, we can learn to make the most of this opportunity and to feel gloriously unshackled by it!

John Dear puts it like this:

> Testifying in a courtroom can be an experience of liberation. The Spirit within us is set free publicly to touch the hearts and minds of others, and in that process, we are empowered to take greater risks and bolder stands for God's truth of love and justice for the poor. We become even more shameless in our passion for the reign of God.[8]

Moreover, several big wins have, in fact, been achieved in the courts. These are important, not because of the individuals concerned but because it signifies that the message about the critical situation we are in is getting heard.

In Autumn 2021, two of the four groups of protesters who had climbed onto DLR trains in 2019 were acquitted, even though a significant disruption had been caused to commuters in and around Canary Wharf. Two separate juries concluded that the disruption was proportionate to the extreme emergency to which the protesters sought to draw attention.

CCA founding member Phil Kingston, giving his evidence over video link in one of these trials, spoke about the terrible losses being sustained by indigenous peoples in the Amazon and of the Amazon Forest itself. Berta Caceres, the Honduran indigenous leader who was awarded the Goldman Environmental prize, was assassinated eleven months later.

The judge did not allow Phil to show the video of Berta, or to read from the transcript about her, but he did allow Phil's barrister to speak some of it. ("Very disappointing and frustrating for me," Phil said afterwards). Even so, the jury heard the main point that Phil was trying to make about the ruthless nature of those who are exploiting the Amazon for profit, at the expense of the essential natural ecosystems there, and their indigenous human populations. Phil and his two co-defendants, Fr Martin Newell and myself, were acquitted.

Despite causing considerable damage, XR scientists were acquitted for their protest outside the Natural History Museum, and a group of doctors were also acquitted at a trial in November 2022.

Dr Fiona Godlee, Ambassador of the UK Health Alliance on Climate Change—and former Editor in Chief of the British Medical Journal—was a part of the protest on Lambeth Bridge:

> These doctors and health professionals... have acted at all times with enormous professionalism, courage and integrity. Their protest is in a long tradition of nonviolent civil disobedience for causes that seek to improve social justice and, in the case of climate protest, to secure a liveable future for all. By acting as they have done, they are fulfilling their duty of care to their patients and the public, alerting us all to the real and present dangers of the climate crisis and calling on our political leaders to act now to avoid climate catastrophe.[9]

Dr Patrick Hart, a GP, said:

> I'm trying to make a point. It's not about our morning coffee being too milky, it's about the deaths of millions, the loss of

everything we care about, in particular the loss of law and order. The level of disruption we caused was proportionate to the problems we face. I don't want to be arrested, but I accept it as a consequence. I'm heavily invested in the rule of law, and I do this to protect the rule of law. Eighteen King's Counsellors have said that we face the collapse of the rule of law.[10]

## THE WITNESS OF EARLY CHRISTIANS

As Christians, of course, we have the legacy of the early church to help us and we have been left some amazing stories of the faithful witness of the first martyrs, who came from all ranks of society, young and old, women and men; bishops, priests and lay people alike. In the first 300 years of the Church's history, thousands of Christians lost their lives in all sorts of terrible ways; thousands of families were bereaved; thousands spent time in prison—all accounting for their faith, and determinedly following in the footsteps of Jesus.

As Christianity spread through the Empire, a clash with the Roman state became inevitable; the worship of the one God, the Father of Jesus Christ, was incompatible with the polytheistic practices of the Empire and was also a grave threat to civil order.

At his death in AD 14, Augustus Caesar was declared a god. From that moment, there could be absolutely no accommodation between the state and the beliefs of Christians. Christians by definition were held to be treasonous, as they could not worship the emperor as God. And so simply to declare oneself to be a Christian was enough to attract the death penalty. Christians did indeed refuse to do things that citizens of the empire were supposed to do, but it was enough to confess to being a Christian to incur the severest of penalties including death. In 122, Pliny—the Roman governor of Bithynia and Pontus (now in modern Turkey)—wrote to the Emperor Trajan:

> This is the course I have taken with those who are accused before me as Christians. I asked them whether they are Christians, and if they confessed, I asked them a second and a third time with threats of punishment. If they kept to it, I ordered them for execution, for I held no question that whatever it was that they admitted, in any case obstinacy and unbending perversity, deserved to be punished. There were others of the like insanity.[11]

Christians were indeed a threat to the Empire. They were active in proselytising, clear that they could not fight to defend the emperor; they rejected all attempts to make them worship the emperor as god, which for the Romans had become a test of patriotism and a mark of loyalty to the state. It is humbling indeed to realise how solid this opposition was within the church in its first three centuries of existence. Although there were moments of wavering, as under bishop Cyprian of Carthage, in the main, fidelity to the faith and to Jesus as Lord was rock solid, demanding a truly costly renunciation of all things for Christ and for many, of life itself.

## *Ignatius*

Ignatius became Bishop of Antioch in Syria towards the end of the first century. The martyrdom of the first apostles would have taken place only a few years earlier and the persecution of the embryonic church by the Roman authorities was happening everywhere. Ignatius was arrested in the reign of Trajan and condemned to fight with wild beasts.

We know a good deal about Ignatius' personal struggles as he was taken overland from Syria to Rome.[12] The fears and misgivings he experienced as he approached his destination humanises him for us. During the stops along the way, Christians gathered to greet him, pray and celebrate the Eucharist. During his journey to Rome, Ignatius wrote seven letters in which he describes his spiritual journey and inner feelings. As he got nearer to Rome and martyrdom, he commented, "Now is the moment I am beginning to be a disciple" and again "We have not only to be called Christians but to *be* Christians." Ignatius believed it to be his primary responsibility as bishop to strengthen the faith of his flock, and his greatest fear was to scandalise them by wavering from his calling to witness to Jesus and to His resurrection. Ignatius died faithfully in the amphitheatre in Rome in 107.

## *Polycarp*

Polycarp, Bishop of Smyrna (western Turkey) was, like Ignatius, one of the first generation of Bishops, receiving his faith and authority from the Apostles. According to tradition, Polycarp was a disciple of John the evangelist. As a young man, he had kissed the chains of Ignatius as he passed through Smyrna on his way to martyrdom in Rome. In a letter to Polycarp, Ignatius commented "A Christian does not control his own life but gives his whole time to God."

Polycarp met his own martyrdom in or around 155, and the account of it given in a letter from the church at Smyrna is the oldest account of Christian martyrdom outside the New Testament. When arrested at the age of 86, he had been a bishop for many decades. Urged by the Roman consul to acknowledge Caesar as Lord and to curse Christ, Polycarp famously replied, "Eighty-six years I have served Him and He never did me any wrong. How can I blaspheme my King who saved me?"[13]

## *Cyprian*

Cyprian was born in north Africa around 210. A senior and influential lawyer, he was converted to Christianity when he was in his mid thirties and was soon ordained deacon and priest and became Bishop of Carthage (modern Tunisia) around 247.

In early 249 the persecutions began. Emperor Decian issued an edict ordering sacrifices to the gods to be made throughout the

Empire. The African church had suffered severely during an earlier persecution, and many Christians had renounced their faith and done homage to the Emperor as god. Cyprian, too, had gone into hiding.

However, Cyprian now tried to prepare his people for the expected edict of persecution by his *De exhortatione martyrii*, and set an example to his flock when he was brought before the Roman proconsul in 257. He refused to sacrifice to the pagan deities, and firmly professed Christ as his Lord. On 13 September 258, Cyprian was imprisoned on the orders of the new proconsul, Galerius Maximus. The public examination of Cyprian by Galerius Maximus, on 14 September 258, has been preserved:

**Galerius Maximus:** Are you Thascius Cyprianus?
**Cyprian:** I am.
**Galerius:** The most sacred Emperors have commanded you to conform to the Roman rites.
**Cyprian:** I refuse.
**Galerius:** Take heed for yourself.
**Cyprian:** Do as you are bid; in so clear a case I may not take heed.
**Galerius:** You have long lived an irreligious life, and have drawn together a number of men bound by an unlawful association, and professed yourself an open enemy to the gods and the religion of Rome; and the pious, most sacred and august Emperors ... have endeavoured in vain to bring you back to conformity with their religious observances; whereas therefore you have been apprehended as principal and ringleader in these infamous crimes, you shall be made an example to those whom you have wickedly associated with; the authority of law shall be ratified in your blood.

Galerius then read the sentence of the court from a written tablet: "It is the sentence of this court that Thascius Cyprianus be executed with the sword." To which Cyprian replied: "Thanks be to God."[14]

## *Perpetua and Felicity*

Perhaps the most poignant example of the witness of the early Christian martyrs, again from the Church in Africa, is that of Perpetua and her servant Felicity, and their companions. Their story is captured in a most unusual autobiographical treatise written by Perpetua and completed by one of her companions who catalogued her death and that of her servant Felicity.[15] The story is unusual in several ways: first that it was written at all in this autobiographical form; second that it was written by a woman and is concerned with uniquely feminine challenges; and third in its exposure of her inner struggles with family obligations, often a part of the suffering for those who engage in civil disobedience but which are seldom discussed.

Perpetua, a young woman in her early twenties was the child of a prosperous family living in Carthage. She was presumably married as she had a new-born son, but there is no mention of her husband or of the father of her child. Her mother was a Christian but not her father. She was part of a catechumenate group who had recently been baptised and the group included some of the family's servants or slaves.

Perpetua and her companions are rounded up and put in prison because of their illegal act in converting to Christianity. In the court, the proconsul appeals to her sense of duty towards her aged father and her baby son but Perpetua simply replies "I am a Christian." She and her companions are convicted and sentenced to fight with wild beasts in the amphitheatre.

Perpetua's father visits her and implores her to renounce her faith. Her little son is removed from her and she suffers the emotional pain of this separation as well as the physical pain of her swollen breasts. After the pleading of her brother, the baby is returned and her physical and emotional pain is relieved. She engages in discussion with friends about his future and as she prepares for her death she organises the care of her baby.

Felicity, her servant, is eight months pregnant. Her fear is that she will not be able to die with her mistress and companions as it was illegal to execute a pregnant woman. So she prays for and is granted an early delivery of a baby daughter, whose future must also be planned. When the two women appear naked in the amphitheatre, the crowd recoils from the sight of women whose bodies show so clearly the signs of recent child bearing and so they are given some clothing. Before their deaths, the mistress and her slave embrace, united now in their Christian faith which has removed all distinctions between them.

The story of these martyrs is instructive, even after taking account of the vast gulf between them and us in terms of culture and historical period. Unusually, we are made privy to the complicated demands of family loyalty that confront both Perpetua and Felicity, especially of course in terms of their recent motherhood. It is truly hard to engage with the clarity and purity of Perpetua's unwavering response—"I am a Christian"—knowing what this meant in terms of the consequences for her baby.

The effect of her decision on her father is even more painful, and we are only left to imagine how the women's decisions were experienced by their partners, who do not appear in the story at all. We are likely to feel horror rather than admiration for the women's unwavering fidelity to their newly professed faith. Yet Jesus promised that following Him would often involve conflict within our families, and many climate crisis resisters can attest to the truth of this. It is certainly part of the sacrifice that some resisters are called upon to make.

Many Christian groups have arisen over the centuries, trying to recover the original clarity of the early church: the newly formed churches of the Reformation held this as their primary task; so did the Quakers. It is still part of the task for Christians today, in order to become what it is that God requires us to be: a sign of contradiction to the values of the world, in this uniquely challenging moment in human history; and uncompromising in our adherence to the truth and the clarity of our commitment to our church's nonviolent, prophetic Founder.

*Can't you hear the future weeping? Our love must save the world.*

Ben Okri

*SEVEN*

# THE COST

In giving us the gift of faith, God asks for *all that we have* in return. There are no half measures to being a Christian; it is all or nothing. We are asked to respond to God's love-gift to us by giving ourselves back to God in totality; responding to the total gift of God's self to us with the total gift of ourselves to God. The stories of some of the early Christian martyrs described in the previous chapter bring home to us only too clearly the cost of our commitment to Christ.

Moreover, we can only get near to answering God's loving and beautiful invitation to us, by allowing God to make our response *on our behalf*. As we say in one of our seasonal prayers, "we have no power of ourselves to help ourselves," so God must do all the work, leaving us to undertake the one (apparently simple) task of letting go and giving our consent. We are called to remember that our faith invites us into sacrificial living, and that sacrifice is at the heart of our faith.

Sacrificial living is our response to the one great Sacrifice that Jesus made for us. But sacrifice, for the Christian, is always a response of love, not of duty or compulsion—still less of the seductions of the ego. It is a response to the Love for us that has already been shown. St. Paul reminds us, in no uncertain terms, that sacrifice that does not flow from love is worse than useless. "If I give my body to be burned but have not love, I am like a sounding gong and a clanging cymbal" (1 Cor 13). So for the Christian, the invitation to sacrifice is always a love gift from God, and our response to the invitation is always a love gift back.

Certainly civil disobedience is costly and requires disruption in our own way of life to free ourselves to take it as Fr Martin Newell points out:

> I would ask, what kind of political change do you think is necessary to achieve the change that is needed? I would argue that, at the very least, it is a massive political earthquake, probably beyond anything that has been seen in the West since 1945. Now what is going to create that? How is God going to be able to bring about that kind of change? Do you think that kind of change, in a good direction, has ever happened without a lot of people being willing to put their freedom, their reputation, even their lives, on the line? I'm absolutely sure it hasn't. So if we want God to act, if we want to bring about that change, we have to ask ourselves—are *we* willing to act? Are *we* willing to pray for the courage to act? Are *we* willing to look at what changes we might need to make in our lives to give us enough free space in them to allow God to enable us to act?[1]

If we desire to offer ourselves in some way for the cause, we also need to interrogate this desire. This includes a consideration of the potential violence to the *self*. Jesus does not offer us a risk-free path—and some of what we do may to some extent be harmful, such as fasting, sitting in vigil all night in the rain and the cold, going without sleep in order to pray at home—but such actions are hopefully prompted by love and obedience, and moderated by the support and advice of others.

Civil disobedience is costly. Civil disobedience may emerge out of the "stubborn self," as the political scientist Gene Sharp puts it;[2] but even so, it is costly to the self as it requires the breaking of a taboo—probably long internalised, and guarded (in psychological terms) by the formidable super-ego, fashioned and fortified since earliest childhood. Some pain and guilt may therefore be engendered by breaking through that boundary. It is also costly, especially the first few times, in terms of its fearfulness and threat, as it takes the self into unknown territory and into a fearful place. Being arrested will be a novel experience for most of us. We may have an uncertain sense of how the police will treat us, or what the process entails. Being handcuffed, placed in a police van, taken into a custody suite, finger printed, photographed, DNA checked and then locked in a cell on one's own all take a bit of getting used to!

One activist described it to me like this:

> I am just an ordinary, law-abiding citizen. I don't like the limelight. I don't like being the focus of any attention. Was I scared? Yes, very. I had never been arrested before. But I was more scared about what is happening now on this beautiful planet we all call home... We don't have any more time. For the sake of life on our planet we must do something. I am not going to sit by and say "What else can I do?" or wait for technology to save us. An elderly woman (I had never met her before) and I held each others' hands for strength and courage. She was shaking like a leaf, she felt like a fragile bird in my hands. It looked like the police were going to take me next. I told her she was brave and strong. As I was carried away, I repeatedly heard her say, *"Yes, I am brave and strong, I am brave and strong."*

There is a cost, too, to others and to one's relationships. Parents, children, partners, spouses did not necessarily sign up for all that is involved in having a loved one break the law, albeit for conscience's sake. Friends and family react in different ways—silence, anger, rejection, denial—and those reactions may in turn be painful to bear. One's family and friends may of course experience a sense of pride, but just as likely they will feel bewildered and ashamed and want to distance themselves, just at the point when one most wants their support. Parents may feel distraught and anxious about their son or daughter's employment prospects after conviction; partners may feel angry and ashamed, or anxious about the welfare of the children, especially if the individual is facing a prison sentence and thus may be absent from home for some months.

All of this needs consideration as part of counting the cost of what is involved in breaking the law. It is part of the discernment process in which we must engage before deciding that this is what God is calling us to do.

Whatever we feel that God is calling us to do, we certainly need to engage in a period of training and preparation for doing it. Part of this preparation should involve immersing ourselves in the literature of protest–the classical writers on civil disobedience–Thoreau, Gandhi, King, Day, Berrigan and Dear. There is nothing like reading some of the primary texts such as *Letter from a Birmingham Jail*, or some of Gandhi's great writing on nonviolent resistance, to get inspiration, build confidence and commitment and ground us in nonviolence.*

## LEARNING FROM PAUL

We need also, of course, to learn from scripture and the early church. Some of Jesus' main promises to us were that we would be persecuted; that we would be reviled and misunderstood, and that following Him would create conflict within our families. Jesus also promised us eternal life, of course–but not without cost. The early Church knew from experience that there was a cost to discipleship: a cost to being a Christian (as many Christians still know only too well

—

* The American Peace Movement and Plowshares has yielded rich experience of civil resistance to the weapons industry, which can be applied to climate crisis resistance. Daniel Berrigan has written extensively on the early church's approach to resistance and on his own experience of going to court and spending time in prison (**11**). John Dear has described the witness of lesser-known American activists in his book *The Sacrament of Civil Disobedience* (**12**). For us, as Europeans, we should not neglect the witness and inspiration of those who resisted the evils of Nazism during the Second World War. Bonhoeffer and others of the Confessing Church had to struggle with the dilemmas of compromise, as they sought to remain nonviolent and yet resist the horrors that were being played out before them (**13**). And Etty Hillsum's Diaries give us an entry point into reflecting how to live life immersed in evil and yet resist it with goodness, despite the ever present threat to her personal safety (**14**).

today, who live under regimes which are hostile to the Christian faith).

In his second letter to Timothy, written from prison, Paul writes: "Everyone who wants to live a Godly life in union with Christ Jesus will be persecuted" (2 Tim 3:12). It is an uncompromising statement, and one which the Church, in the West at least, has all but relegated to the reaches of hyperbole or romance. Yet we urgently need to recover how real an experience persecution was for Paul, and how central a part of Christian life he believed it to be.

Throughout the first three centuries, the issue became increasingly clear-cut; conflict with the state became more likely. Christians were perceived to be a threat to public order. Their lifestyle was different, and they actively proselytised. They refused to join the army, which in itself indicated their unwillingness to defend the Emperor or promote his cause.

Christians therefore inevitably became engaged in acts of civil disobedience—but none more so as when they were forced to worship the Emperor as God. Worshipping the Emperor was a test of loyalty as a citizen, and those who could not or would not pass that test, automatically became enemies of the state, and were treated as such. This involved frequent imprisonments and executions; it was said that many people found it so frightening to become a Christian that they would put off being baptised until their death bed!

In the book of Acts, we see the apostles persevering in their work of teaching and healing in the face of strict prohibitions imposed by the Jewish authorities. In Acts 5, the authorities respond—not for the first time—by putting the apostles in jail. But God will not be thwarted; the apostles are released by the intervention of an angel, and immediately return to the Temple to continue their work.

The authorities are baffled as to what to do, as authorities usually are when they encounter such fearless and God-inspired opposition. On Gameliel's advice, they have the apostles whipped and then released, again ordering them never to speak in the name of Jesus again. "As the apostles left the Council they were happy because God had considered them worthy to suffer disgrace for the sake of Jesus. And every day in the Temple and in peoples' homes, they continued to preach the Good News about Jesus the Messiah" (Acts 5:41- 42).

The apostles' resistance to the authorities was unflinching, because for them it was the only way that they could be obedient to God. It required a willingness to walk the way of the cross, knowing that this Way would end for them, as it had for Jesus, in the ultimate gift of their lives. It was, and is, the cost of standing up against evil, and opening up the way of justice and love for all God's children to enjoy.

The Book of Acts continues by describing the witness of Stephen, whose fidelity to Jesus cost him his life. It goes on to describe the way in which Paul, along with his companions Silas and Barnabas, frequently had to choose civil disobedience in order to be faithful to their allegiance to Jesus.

In chapter 16, we find that Paul and Silas are arrested in Philippi and thrown into jail, for teaching customs against the Jewish law. The officials were summoned and ordered Paul and Silas to be whipped, chained and detained in the inner part of the prison. But an earthquake shakes the foundations of the jail and their chains fall off. Terrified, the jailor fears that all his prisoners will have escaped; but having found them still there, he asks Paul and Silas what he must do to be saved. In a wonderful way, their fortitude and transparency is instrumental in bringing their opponent to faith.

And then the denouement. The next morning, the Roman officials are sent to the prison with the order to let Paul and Silas go. "Not likely," replies Paul. "They take us and have us whipped, throw us in prison, even though we are Roman citizens and having found us not guilty, they want us just to leave secretly! No indeed—they must come to the prison and get us out themselves—publicly!" So the Romans went to the prison and apologised to them, and asked them to leave the city!

Paul's courage, persistence and endurance is remarkable. He travels through much of the empire, challenging the worship of the emperor, and of other pagan gods, with the worship of God, as He is revealed in Jesus. This is upsetting to the ordinary population as well as to those who earn their living from making idols to the great goddess Diana (as they do in Athens).

Finally, Paul arrives back in Jerusalem. The apostles report to him the divisions he has caused amongst the converted Jews, because of the way in which they perceive Paul as having allowed Gentile converts to abandon important Jewish customs—notably circumcision. Paul's arrival in the Temple causes a riot; he is mobbed and attacked, until a Roman commander arrests Paul and takes him into the fort.

Paul asks for permission to address the people and—notwithstanding the manhandling and beating he has just received—he tells the crowd the story of his conversion from having been a zealous persecutor of followers of the Way, to now wanting to preach the Good News that Jesus of Nazareth is the Messiah, for whom the Jews have waited so long.

As he has done before, Paul challenges his captors. "Is it lawful for you to whip a Roman citizen who hasn't even been tried for any crime?" The Romans withdraw, later taking Paul before the Chief priest and Council to find out what Paul was accused of. Paul cleverly exploits the divisions between Sadducees and Pharisees, but the unrest continues and Paul is again removed into the fort and remains under arrest.

Saved by his nephew from a plot to kill him, Paul is safely taken by the soldiers to the Governor Felix in Caesarea by night; this enables him to plead his cause—and in the process inform the Governor and the Governor's staff and guard about the Gospel of Jesus that he is preaching. Again, Paul takes the initiative: he appeals to the Emperor for the justice he deserves. From then on, Paul remained in custody, eventually being transported to Rome, where he remained under house arrest for two years.

He may also have been in prison while in Rome, as he suggests in his second letter to Timothy (1:16) when he commends Onesiphorus for not being ashamed that he, Paul, was in prison. Tradition has it that he was eventually executed by Nero during a period of escalated persecution of Christians, when the crucial challenge had to be faced: the followers of Jesus could not also worship the Emperor as god, pay him taxes or be conscripted into taking part in his violent and oppressive wars. The followers of Jesus had espoused a different way of life—a life of nonviolence, service and love.

The mission of Paul repays careful study: it has much to teach those of us who feel called to participate in acts of civil disobedience at this time of climate crisis. Like Peter, Paul demonstrates by his life, as well as by his words, that following Jesus will usually involve being misunderstood and often hated. His actions, and ours, will cause division, even among those who are active in the cause of bringing in God's Kingdom.

Our calling into civil disobedience may also cause division in our families and amongst our friends, and will incur for us the drudgery of court appearances and their preparation, the inconvenience of spending time in police custody and the fearfulness of going to prison for the first time. Paul exemplifies how to go about it all! He is fearless in the face of opposition, accepting of the consequences of his actions, strong in his response to those who try to treat him inappropriately and perfectly prepared to stand up for his rights against authority.

Yet: he is caring to all whom he encounters, anxious for the wellbeing of the jailor who thought his prisoners had escaped (and in fact, brings him to faith) and delighted to use the opportunities he is afforded when under arrest and in prison to preach the Good News by his words and his example. Like Jesus, Paul is strong and immovable in his witness to truth, but nonviolent, compassionate and concerned for those with whom he becomes involved.

## FACING PRISON

It seems to come as a shock to the average church member that several of Paul's letters were written from prison; that arrest and imprisonment was a regular feature of the life of many first century Christians and that even to be a Christian was a contravention of the law.

Fr Martin Newell, a founder member of CCA, imprisoned for his action with Ploughshares, writes about prison as follows:

> Risking time in prison is something that some of us, at least, judge to be a necessary response to the climate and environmental emergency. If that is something we are going to experience, then reflecting on the experience from the perspective of faith—to try to make some deeper sense of that difficult time, that sacrifice—can give us strength to face up to it, to risk it, and to come through it with our faith and our humanity strengthened, not diminished. I hope that sharing our reflections, in faith and love, can encourage and inspire others not to be afraid to take the risks required [including going to prison] to help bring about the enormous, deep, drastic and urgent ecological, spiritual and political conversion that is required in these times.[3]

A preparedness to go to prison for the sake of conscience and faith, and in obedience to God's purposes as we discern them, is a significant sacrifice. As such, this sacrifice has the potential for being extremely fruitful in our Christian discipleship and for our witness to the climate crisis. We can offer it back to God with joy, for God to use in the work of bringing in the Kingdom of justice and peace on earth. By going to prison, we are following Jesus to the end point of His Passion, short of dying with Him.

In the UK, going to prison is the ultimate penalty for standing up for what is right against the forces of evil. Whilst not to be compared with facing the death penalty, it is still a significant sanction, and one from which most of us will shy away. It involves the complete loss of liberty and control over our lives and the deprivation of those things we are likely to hold most dear: family, friends, freedom and all the many activities with which our lives are usually filled.

It may also be the moment when family and friends who have stuck by us so far find prison to be one step beyond what they can accept, making it all the harder for the individual to gather the courage and strength to face this next stride forward in discipleship. Climate crisis resistance is so recent, we have had little to draw upon as yet in terms of experience of prison other than quite short stays—usually on remand awaiting trial, or handed down as punishment for contempt of court.*

Otherwise, we have mostly to look to others to learn from their experience, especially those who have a long grounding in the peace movement. Fr. Martin Newell speaks of the spiritual power of going to prison for the cause of justice and truth: "One of the strange things about being in prison is that, just by being there, not by necessarily doing anything, it can be a very powerful and significant act. As Phil Berrigan, the American peace activist said, "prison speaks to conscience" as does all willingness to suffer voluntarily for what is right. Or so I believe. It is about the power of voluntary suffering, of sacrifice, for the sake of love which of course is something very much tied in with our faith, with my understanding of the cross of Jesus and how it brings conversion. Because conversion is what is needed above all—both an ecological conversion, and a political one, in the broadest possible sense of the word 'political'."[4]

Imprisonment is the ultimate handing over, the fullest expression of the loss of our liberty, and the final statement of a nonviolent

---

* However in April 2023, Morgan Trowland and Marcus Decker were sentenced to a period of 3 years, and 2 years and 7 months respectively, for disrupting traffic by climbing on top of the Queen Elizabeth bridge and closing the bridge for 41 hours. (**15**)

act. Thus it brings us most fully into confrontation with the violent, destructive activity of the state, hellbent on climate chaos, war and the prioritisation of profit over people. We are called to be faithful in opposing this evil. We see this immoveable fidelity in the early church: Christ had total claim upon His disciples, and this required the fullest commitment from his followers to resist evil in all its forms, even when this required the total loss of their/our liberty.*

Several of St. Paul's letters were written in prison (and others,† which may have been written by his followers, were set in the context of his imprisonment)—thus giving the imprimatur to the early church's acceptance of the need for, and purposefulness of imprisonment. Many of his companions followed him to prison during his ministry. Prison was, for Paul, an inevitable consequence of preaching the Gospel.

Paul clearly saw the positive value of being in prison. In his letter to the Philippians he writes:

> I want you to know, my brothers and sisters, that the things that have happened to me have really helped the progress of the Gospel. As a result, the whole Palace Guard and all the others here know that I am in prison because I am a servant of Christ. And my being in prison has given most of the brothers and sisters more confidence in the Lord, so that they grow bolder all the time to preach the message fearlessly.
> *Philippians 1:12-14*

Many protesters who go to prison—or even taste the possibility of prison by being incarcerated for some hours in a police cell—speak of it as a profound experience. I do not want to romanticise something that is mundane and disagreeable, and experienced painfully by many

---

* We have strayed so far from any understanding of the Christian witness of imprisonment, or even of the value of civil disobedience in general that two Bishops in the Church of England announced in 2021 that they "could not condone breaking the law."

† Colossians and Ephesians

of the population every day, often for no good reason at all. Yet for the Christian it may lead to unique discoveries in one's spiritual life.

Being deprived of one's liberty in this way can be an experience of profound insight and closeness to God. This is because it has the potential for deepening our dependency on God, all other props having been removed. The experience costs us not less than everything; at first glance, and in reality, it is a profound humiliation. But in the loving acceptance of the humiliation of it all, there opens up a significant gateway into the deep humility which, in our best moments, we know to be fundamental to all spiritual growth. We may also experience the great peace and certainty of knowing that we are doing God's will. And all of this brings deep gratitude.

Everyone who is arrested is taken to a custody suite, and can be held for up to 24 hours. Protesters find the experience varies tremendously depending upon the staff and facilities at each venue; but whatever the details of the experience, being detained and locked up in a cell means being deprived of one's liberty and much of one's agency to influence events. It may be experienced as a humiliation—being strip searched for example—and it may reveal how far one is from the kind of humility shown by Jesus in the face of the most degrading and abusive of experiences which He underwent.

I recall that at one of the custody suites where I was taken, we were given no water, nor a blanket, for several hours after arriving—when we were very cold, wet and inevitably stressed by the action and the arrest. I felt angry; when I was released, I complained of the treatment we had received.

My fellow arrestees, who—unlike me—had also been strip-searched, looked at me blankly. I realised how far I was from accepting our treatment in the way we had committed ourselves to do, as part of our nonviolent response to whatever came our way and in solidarity with those in other countries (and sometimes in our own) who are treated so much worse than those of us who hold inherent privilege. I realised, too, that even being strip-searched was no more than Jesus had undergone. Why should His disciples expect anything better?

## APPROACHES TO PRISON TIME

There are several ways in which protesters tend to approach the experience of prison. The first is to view incarceration as a continuation of the action, and stage various kinds of protests and acts of civil disobedience in prison. The second is to rebel against what may seem an unwarrantable interference in one's human rights, for which professional help must be sought and the legal system contested. The third might be called the Gandhian approach, whereby one receives one's prison sentence with equanimity, accepting the judgement of the court and the subsequent arrangements made for one's incarceration. Those adopting such an approach might sum it up, in the words of one member of CCA as: "Expect nothing; be grateful for anything."

Another approach is to see prison as a means of avoiding complicity with the state which is responsible for the evil which one is contesting. Prison affords one the opportunity of stepping outside the system altogether, and living in a kind of parallel universe, using the time creatively and productively and offering up the many privations for God to use in the relief of the suffering of others. However lacking in success an action may seem to have been in achieving a particular goal, it is always within our power to achieve our goal to some degree by refusing complicity with the evil perpetrated by the state. This endows the experience of going to prison with a power that cannot be removed, however powerless a person is in all other respects.

Thoreau viewed prison in this light. Although he was only in prison for one night, he wrote about his experience and the reasons for taking such a course of action in such a way that his example has had a special impact on all later discussion of the topic. Thoreau saw prison as the ultimate refusal to be complicit with an unjust, corrupt or neglectful regime; a way of stepping outside society and withdrawing one's consent from it.[5]

Reparation may provide another motivation: making reparation for one's own complicity in the climate crisis by the lifestyle one has led in the past or which one continues to live now, contributing to the causes of the crisis. A further way of valuing incarceration in prison is to see it as a way of preparing for the draconian system of control over our lives which will be required when we are having to live beyond a 3 degree rise in temperature. It will be hard indeed for those used to the freedoms of a democratic society to embrace the many strictures which will have to be imposed by a continuous "war time" regime. Those who have experienced prison may be able to offer help and support and hope.

For Gandhi, Martin Luther King and for so many others, the power of the witness of going to prison was in its acceptance of suffering in order to avoid inflicting suffering on others. The redemptive power of suffering is demonstrated by going to prison. The call to hear the profound truth of a situation is revealed by those who are prepared to accept this ultimate sanction and considerable sacrifice. If one is prepared to go to prison for one's beliefs, so the argument goes, they surely must be worth listening to.

Nevertheless, time spent in prison may be experienced as very desolate, and the individual may suffer from depression and anxiety throughout his or her stay. Such a painful experience can still be made fruitful if it is offered to God for the purposes of the civil resistance in which the individual is engaged. Gandhi placed high value on the individual making his or her time in prison as productive and purposeful as possible. In his own case he developed a regime of exercise, study, meditation, writing and prayer as well as outreach to his fellow prisoners and to the staff. John Dear comments that once in prison, "we can still speak out about the issues of justice and peace through our prayers, love and outreach."[6]

Perhaps Mandela's greatest achievement while in prison was to make enduring friendships with several of the prison guards. His long period of detention was usable as a preparation for the future—a future which turned out to include the leadership of his country, away from an apartheid regime into the uncharted waters of a multiracial state.[7]

The experience of spending time in prison does need to be made as productive as it possibly can be, to help it be meaningful both for the individual and for the cause and for the struggle itself. Dietrich Bonhoeffer, a German Lutheran theologian and pastor, spent 18 months in prison after his complicity in the plot to overthrow Hitler was suspected. During that time, he continued his theological work, and wrote a large number of letters and articles which, after his execution, were collected together under the title *Letters and Papers from Prison*, and published posthumously in 1951. Even though conditions were spartan, he had access to books and he was able to communicate with others, sending and receiving written material.

Such access is often denied prisoners today because of the fear of drugs being smuggled into prison, which means that prisoners may be denied all access to books and writing materials for a considerable period of time. Fortunately for us, this was not the case for Bonhoeffer. Bonhoeffer studied theology before the war and in 1937, he published what was probably his best known book, *The Cost of Discipleship,* which has been an inspiration to many in taking their faith seriously enough to answer the call to the sacrifices required in confronting an evil or neglectful regime.*

Daniel Berrigan spent two years in Danbury Federal Prison in the

---

* His writings on Christianity's role in the secular world have become widely influential both in the West and on liberation theologians. Bonhoeffer's witness against the horrors of the Nazi regime had been profound and unflinching. The regime had, of course, been the legal government of Germany and Bonhoeffer's opposition had therefore been one of civil disobedience. It is a stark and timely reminder that just because a government is 'legal' it may not be moral, responsible or concerned for the common good of its people. Sometimes, it may have to be opposed.

US, beginning in August 1970, for his participation in the Cantonsville Nine draft board raid against the US war in Vietnam. On October 20, 1970, he listed his hopes and prayers in his prison diary, and the insights gained from prison life:

> That what we do, what we endure, will have meaning for others. That our lives are not wasted, in the measure in which we give them. That the giving of our lives is a concrete, simple task; at center eye, the men we live with and suffer among and strive to serve. That life in jail, in proportion to one's awareness, has powerful analogies with "life outside" to the inquiring mind and the contemplative heart. That to be fools for Christ's sake is a responsible political position, given the rampant death society, its irresponsibility and horror of life. That we are called, as prisoners, to be disciplined, prayerful, constant, vigilant over sense and appetite, cheerful and of good heart. That relief of inequity, inhumanity, and injustice are present and pressing tasks. The struggle goes on here too.
> That powerlessness is a way which offers solidarity and concurrent action with all those who struggle and endure in the world. That in prison we are in communion not only with suffering men and women of our world, but with the communion of saints in every time and place. That our jailers also lie under the scrutiny as well as the saving will of God, and stand in great need of our compassion and our courtesy... That we are called to live the mystery of the cross and to sweat through the mystery of the resurrection. That we accept first, in body and spirit, our conviction that human conditions must worsen, that there is more to be endured than we have so far endured, before amelioration comes. That good humor and riding easy are the saving salt of our condition. We may win big, we may win small, we may lose everything. We can take whichever outcome. Important: stand where you must stand, be human there.[8]

"In a true sense," Berrigan wrote a few weeks later, "it can be said of Philip [his brother] and me that we have nothing to do but stand firm in these months—to survive, to act as a silent prick to the consciences of those outside whether of friend or opponent, church or state."[9]

"How to believe that our being here is making a difference for others?" he asked himself on March 16, 1971.

> We are to believe, as I do most firmly, that being here is the natural crown of everything that went before; not merely in a humanistic sense that good people inevitably come to ill, but in the sense of the crowning of a journey of faith by the opening of a wider vista of faith. The reward of faith, that is to say, is not vision, it is a life which both requires and bestows a greater measure of faith; the ability to see the journey through, stage by stage, so that the promise, still withheld, remains itself, pristine, never cancelled.

"I feel at peace, a strange feeling, one to be grateful for while it lasts."[10] So much of Daniel Berrigan's writings repay a time of deep consideration and reflection.

"The ability to see the journey through, stage by stage..." That is indeed the challenge faced now by those engaged in civil resistance to catastrophic climate change. We have to be prepared to be in it for the long haul. There will be different phases to this period of resistance, with the certainty that those intent upon holding on to business as usual will become more and more determined to push back against us. Prison sentences will get longer and harsher; those opposed to us being involved in civil resistance will become angrier and more hostile. This is the challenge we are called upon to face. An effort to discover and silence the "ringleaders" of the radical parts of the movement has already led the police to get charges of conspiracy to succeed in some courts with some prominent members of Just Stop Oil being incarcerated in the worst prisons for considerable lengths of time.

For climate protesters who, in this country, have as yet little experience of prison, learning that prison is nevertheless "doable" is the important lesson for us all. CCA member Sue Hampton was remanded in custody at Bronzefield prison after JSO's special Injunction-breaking action designed to get all participants in prison at once in September 2022. Some who had prepared for this action—around 80 in all—had dropped out because of the clash with the period of national mourning taking place for the Queen, but 51 remained and the action successfully got all 51 in prison. At the end of the tough first day, when she had spent many hours in court cells, police vans and the prison reception area, Sue wrote in her prison diary: "I knew I could do this, and I knew that people must."

As the government fights back with more and more draconian penalties and as the courts seem only marginally willing to stand up to government pressure, activists have to consider at greater depth what longer prison sentences might mean. At present, the charge of public nuisance—with which some Insulate Britain protesters have been charged—attracts a maximum penalty of ten years. No climate protester in the UK as yet has had to consider how that would play out in their life. No one as yet has had to contemplate the length of sentence endured by Nelson Mandela, incarcerated on Robben Island for 27 years, or that of Gandhi, or that of Jessica Reznicek sentenced in the United States during the summer of 2022 for a term of eight years for damaging an oil pipeline.

It seems as though God may be calling us now to a much higher level of commitment and sacrifice, which feels both realistic and frightening in equal measure: realistic because the power, determination and evil of the fossil fuel industry and its supporting financial institutions are formidable; frightening because we are staring into the abyss of unlimited fines and court costs and hugely augmented prison sentences. But Jesus has said "Whoever shall endure to the end shall be saved." The call to deep prayer has never been more urgent: to inspire a new generation of civil resisters, and help us gain and retain the moral strength and courage we need to continue to resist the greatest challenge humanity has ever faced.

*To serve as custodians of creation is not an empty title; it requires that we act, and with all the urgency that this dire situation requires.*

Desmond Tutu

*To care enough to act we need a spiritual awakening.*

Words on a banner at a Vigil outside Parliament

*I do this not because I know it's going to work but because I don't know its not going to work.*

Jimmy Thomas, a member of Insulate Britain
and Just Stop Oil.

*EIGHT*

# DO YOU THINK IT'S GOING TO WORK?

Awareness of the ecological and climate crises amongst the general public and amongst our political representatives has increased of late, with more than 75% of the public saying they are either concerned or very concerned. Yet we still stand back from the full meaning of what our increasing awareness implies. Denial of what is happening is still the prevalent response to the climate crisis. The understanding of the likely consequences of climate, ecological and civilisation collapse remains scant, and the political will to focus on it effectively is clearly absent—let alone the desire to engage with the far-reaching social, industrial and economic reforms required.

Philosopher and political scientist Frédéric Gros asks, in his book entitled *Disobey*,

> Why have we said nothing in the face of imminent catastrophe? Why do we still remain today with dangling arms and our eyes trying — I won't even say resigned — to look elsewhere? Why have we let this happen; why have we behaved like spectators of the disaster?... Those who come after us will convict us of a demented egoism, a deadly irresponsibility.[1]

What is wrong with us? Why do we not do what needs to be done? There is more than one reason, but Naomi Klein believes "the answer is far more simple than many have led us to believe: we are stuck because the actions that would give us the best chance of averting this catastrophe—and would benefit the vast majority—are extremely threatening to an elite minority that has a stranglehold over our economy, our political process and most of our major media outlets."[2]

"I think one of the reasons why people are in such denial is because there is a culture of *un-care*," says Sally Weintrobe, Chair of the International Psychoanalytical Association's Committee on Climate Change. She argues that neoliberalism has boosted a sense of exceptionalism, damaged our sense of social responsibility to one another—making us all 'consumers'—and seeded the bubble of denial around climate change.[3]

Undoubtedly too, in 2023 (the time of writing), human beings are now faced with several interlocking crises which can feel nothing short of paralysing. We have a cost of living crisis, with rampant inflation; the Covid pandemic is far from over in the world; the climate crisis (as the most recent IPCC report observed in February 2022) is more critical than ever and, with the outbreak of war between Russia and Ukraine, the world has edged nearer to an all out nuclear confrontation than since the 60s.

In the UK, our current government is showing less grasp of reality, less determination and less willingness to act than any previous administration. A vast new coal mine in Cumbria has been given the go-ahead;* green levies on fuel bills have been eliminated; hundreds of new licences have been issued for prospecting for new oil off the north west coast of Scotland; the ban on fracking was lifted but thankfully reinstated. Our own Climate Change Committee assesses that "continuing with existing policies is likely to result in around 2.7 °C of warming"[4]—a figure which is likely to lead to an unlivable planet.

Although nations at COP26 agreed not to support new fossil fuel projects in the developing world, the UK will continue to fund the

—

* The mine will be responsible for millions of tonnes of carbon emissions and will produce the most polluting grade of coal. The British government apparently feels that as most of the coal will be exported, it does not matter that the pollution from it will be high, as though the atmosphere is divided up between national borders by some line in the sky!

massive new gas project in Mozambique—because this is categorised as a "legacy project." Since COP26, and with the outbreak of war in Ukraine, the Government appears to be rowing back from even its minimal commitment to a net zero carbon goal by 2050, the perceived need for new fossil fuels "in the short term" making the likelihood of reducing carbon emissions in the UK impossible.

For the fossil fuel industry, the war in Ukraine seems like an answer to prayer, just when the industry was beginning to think that the opposition was making its case quite effectively! What a fortuitous gift! To become independent of Russia and other fossil fuel producing states, it is argued, the UK must urgently develop its own. Gas, oil and coal are all potentially to be exploited once more and the Government has issued many new licences to enable this to begin,* with the closing of coal fired power stations, projected for 2024, now to be delayed.[5]

Such abnegation of responsibility by the governments of the world, in the face of such threats to the well being of the human and non-human populations of the planet, surely invites acts of nonviolent civil disobedience in response. Or put another way, it is hard to see how we will get governments to turn around and address this unique existential crisis, with the urgency that is required, without a sustained use of civil disobedience.

To paraphrase Greta Thunberg, it is no use focusing on what is politically possible; we must focus on what needs to be done. When governments are in dereliction of their duty, citizens have both the right and the duty to oppose them, which was a point made by Dr Rowan Williams and other theologians and academics, writing to the

---

* The momentum for this U-turn is so great that it is hard to get any hearing at all for the alternative view that the time lag in producing fossil fuels from scratch is years, whereas the renewable energy industry—solar, wind and tide—needs only to be bolstered with massive injections of cash, to enable the production of all the energy we need, without having to be dependent on anyone else at all—and to do so in short order and for all time to come.

*Guardian*, in October 2018:

> When a government wilfully abrogates its responsibility to protect its citizens from harm and to secure the future for generations to come, it has failed in its most essential duty of stewardship. The "social contract" has been broken, and it is therefore not only our right, but our moral duty to bypass the government's inaction and flagrant dereliction of duty, and to rebel to defend life itself.[6]

When governments become neglectful of their duty, self-serving, corrupt, ignorant or malevolent, they become the "powers and principalities" of which St. Paul spoke. In our current dire situation of impending climate catastrophe, when human beings are being led to the brink of the abyss, many Christians agree with Dr. Rowan Williams and his associates and view the inaction or perverse negative action of governments on climate change as a breach of their social contract with their citizens. This, in turn, invites a response of withdrawal of consent to be governed.

"All governments rely on co-operation and obedience for their very existence," Gene Sharp wrote in his highly influential book *The Politics of Nonviolent Action*. "When people choose to withhold or withdraw that co-operation, governments are left without any pillars to support their weight."[7]

## BEARING FRUIT

I notice, however, that encouraging people to step up to this particular plate seems to be a lot more difficult now than in the heady days of the peace movement, and the effort to get nuclear weapons abolished. Few people, even in this immensely serious and terrifying situation, are prepared to break the law to demand government action. Why? As Gros asks, "[W]hat makes it so hard to contravene, refuse, transgress, even when we have justice on our side? Respect for authority? Fear of the consequences? Fidelity to an initial commitment? Terror of being isolated, stigmatised, pointed out? Or merely just passive inertia?"[8]

No doubt all of these, in varying degrees. Civil disobedience is, for most people, such an unusual, countercultural, potentially terrifying activity that it requires some further comment. Acts of civil disobedience are often bizarre, outrageous and, to the onlooker, just "off the wall." They are inexplicable, crazy, wacky. Sometimes there is an obvious link between the action that we are protesting about, sometimes not.

Many people's reaction to those taking acts of civil disobedience is one of hostility. Sometimes this hostility, when expressed to the protesters sitting on a road, can be changed, as it was for our lorry driver on the M25 described at the opening of this book. Quite often hostility can be lessened, or changed completely, through discussion in a neutral and accepting environment such as a climate cafe—when the hostile person can learn more about climate science and the reasons for the protesters' extreme actions.

More people are simply curious. "Why are you doing this?" can be a perfectly open, genuine question. Why indeed! For most people looking on, we must be doing what we are doing because we think our actions will be effective in changing government policy or public opinion. Thus, "do you think it's going to work" is an obvious question for us to be asked. But the answer is not so obvious! As a rule, we do not know whether an action is likely to be effective; nor, more fundamentally, do we know how we would measure or assess its efficacy anyway.

Of course, we try to take the action that is most effective in arriving at the goal of creating change; and in order to do this we study movements of social change from the past, to learn what seems to work. We prepare for, and construct the action in order to give it the best chance of a successful outcome; the research of psychologists and sociologists, examining the effects of different kinds of protest, is to be welcomed. Actions need to be well prepared and well explained to the media in advance. The demands being made on the Government need to be simple and doable.*

What is clear from history, too, is that in the face of government opposition and frightening intransigence, *only* a sustained campaign of civil disobedience has ever had any chance of bringing about the change that is required. Yet whether our actions are effective or not—important as that is—may not be our first consideration. We are probably having to act before understanding every aspect of our action and its consequences. We are doing what we are doing because, as we see it, it is simply the right thing—and the only thing left—to do.

It may take a long time for acts of civil disobedience to bear ultimate fruit in terms of the hopes and aspirations of the protesters. We do what we do in the hope that those who witness the action will see that we believe so passionately in the truth of what the scientists are saying, and what that means for the speed and severity of the impending catastrophe that we are prepared to risk everything to try to get governments and people to listen and take action.

Perhaps, along the way, these acts may subtly shift the landscape and prepare the ground for ultimate success, even though they may appear fruitless, useless, or even counterproductive at the time. By our jarring, unexpected, law-breaking actions we are trying to break the spell that is mesmerising the world, and keeping peoples and governments paralysed, unable to do what needs to be done. But in the last analysis, the more important consideration is that, for the individual, the action is the right thing to do. He or she believes that they can do no other.

---

* The demand of Just Stop Oil, for example, is simple: keep all new fossil fuels in the ground. Their protests are making a direct link between stopping the flow of oil by blocking tankers, and the need to end the use of this fossil fuel.

## INSULATE BRITAIN

In 2021, we saw a regrouping and re-energising of the climate movement after the inevitable pause imposed by the pandemic. The G7 gathering in Carbis Bay found XR and Christian Climate Action ready and waiting to call the leaders of the richest nations to account; the world was looking towards the next meeting of COP in Glasgow in November.

In the run up to COP26, a new group formed—Insulate Britain—designed to make the simple no-brainer demand that the British housing stock be insulated, starting with the homes of the poorest, and that this should be funded by the government. This would cut carbon emissions by 15%; save at least 8,000 deaths a year in people's own homes from cold (the 2020 assessment)[9], and provide good quality jobs for a newly recruited and well-trained workforce.

Having made this demand—to which the government did not respond—the organisers of Insulate Britain mounted a campaign of two months' continuous civil disobedience and disruption, targeting motorways around London and bringing traffic to a halt by sitting on the carriageways.

The Insulate Britain Campaign was, not surprisingly, hugely unpopular with the public. By stepping into the carriageway of motorways (or slip roads leading to them), the protesters caused significant delays to motorists and commercial traffic. The campaign lasted for around 2 months, from September 15th to November 4th, with a pause during half-term. People felt angry, and baffled as to what connection there was between the group's demand of the government to insulate the 29 million homes in the UK, and their action in sitting on the motorway.

For those taking part, there were several clear connections. The act of disrupting "business as usual" was in itself a prototype of what has to happen in our fossil fuel-addicted society. It also flagged up the fact that the government had set aside £27 billion for motorway expansion and repair—when the use of road transport has to diminish—as compared with the withdrawal of grants for the insulation of homes.

A more subtle connection was also being made: between those who could afford to travel by car to well paid jobs in the City, and those who are far removed from such possibilities, in our grossly unequal society; those without cars, in fuel poverty, at the very bottom of the economic ladder. Tackling inequality in society is part of attending to the climate crisis, as a hugely disproportionate amount of carbon emissions are produced by the rich (and the very rich).

Fundamentally, though, the disruption caused to the public by an hour or so of delay—inconvenient and regrettable as this was—did not bear comparison to the disruption that is coming down the line as a result of climate breakdown. It was a matter of proportion, and it was important to try to convey this message.

Can we imagine what disruption will be caused to our way of life when the climate catastrophe finally hits the UK, Europe, and the US in a more recognisable way than it has done so far? At the beginning of the Covid pandemic, we saw people fighting for toilet rolls in supermarkets. What will it be like when we are fighting for food, or even more, for water? We see what it is like now in some African countries, in Syria, in Palestine.

What will it be like when our heating and lighting fail; when huge areas—the whole of London for example—are flooded; when vast areas of our forest and moorland are on fire; when our air pollution is causing thousands more deaths than it already does now; when people fleeing from drought stricken areas of the world are hammering on the doors of Europe and the UK even more loudly and more insistently than they are now, because it is still *just* possible to live here, but not there?

What will it be like to be confronted by our children and grandchildren asking why we did not listen to the science of climate change before it was too late? By comparison with all of these imminent nightmares, causing a small and temporary disruption on the motorways is hardly worth noticing–other than to beg the government that they act on the symbolism of that disruption, pause business as usual, and reverse the current spending priorities of £27 billion on motorway expansion compared with nothing at all on insulating our homes.[10] As Dr Rowan Williams put it when interviewed at an interfaith gathering in London to show repentance for climate sin, "if you're really angry and put off by the actions of protesters, what exactly are *you* doing? What are *you* going to do to turn all this around?"[11]

If you're wondering what happened next: the Government intervened in the Court system towards the end of 2021, to ensure that Insulate Britain protesters were first tried in the civil court and could then be charged with contempt of court for breaking Injunctions that had, by then, been imposed. This resulted in the first nine protesters who were tried, being sent to prison; Ben Taylor for six months, the others for three. Thereafter, the other defendants were given suspended prison sentences and enormous court costs.

A year later, we were all taken through the criminal courts, charged with either wilful obstruction of the highway or the more serious charge of public nuisance. The Public Order Act which passed in April 2023 increased the scope and severity of the sentences for disruptive protest; the UN Commissioner for Human Rights promptly called on the UK Government to reverse it.[12]

However, the hoped-for effect of getting groups of protesters into prison–with a subsequent sympathy swing in their favour–did not materialise. The sacrifice offered by dozens of protesters from all walks of life seemed to go unheeded, largely because it got almost no mention in the press. The public seemed unaware that there were consequences to sitting on a motorway and getting arrested, which could lead to heavy fines and also imprisonment.

Nonetheless, the relentless cycle of road blocks–interspersed with other unexpected and unusual protests–seemed to be having an effect; as did the resolute determination of the protesters, returning again and again to block roads after being arrested and held for hours in police and court cells. A whole range of organisations declared their support.* On October 24th, the *Guardian* reported that 66% of the public now support direct action to draw attention to the climate crisis.[13]

A YouGov poll released in early June 2019 had already shown that "the environment" ranked in the public's top three most important issues for the first time. Pollsters concluded that the "sudden surge in concern is undoubtedly boosted by the publicity raised for the environmental cause by Extinction Rebellion [which had occupied prominent sites in central London for two weeks in 2019].[14]

There is also evidence from researchers at Bristol University led by Professor Colin Davis that home insulation has risen up the policy agenda since Insulate Britain's protests"—quite some achievement for a movement of only 100 people. Davis suggests that the attention gained from radical actions may, at times, seem to miss the intended "issue" by focusing more on what the protesters are doing. Nonetheless, "protest plays a role in agenda seeding." It influences people's thoughts and moves them towards engagement with the issue of climate change maybe for the first time.[15]

In the UK print media, following the Insulate Britain campaign,the number of mentions of the word "insulation" (not "Insulate") doubled. And a very concrete event—whether causally related to the Insulate Britain campaign or not—was the fact that in his Autumn statement (November 2022), the Chancellor set aside £6 billion towards the insulation of the 29 million homes that make up the United Kingdom's housing stock.

Members of CCA and other Christians have joined in actions by

---

* Members of Christian Climate Action held a Eucharist outside Downing Street to pray for the government (to take action); and vigils were held outside Westminster Cathedral, whilst many CCA members joined JSO on the roads.

both Insulate Britain and Just Stop Oil, and are welcome members of the campaigns. Do we think it's going to work? The answer, I believe, is a resounding "yes"! Somewhat to people's surprise, all political parties, other than the Conservatives, have committed in recent months to issuing no new licences to explore or excavate for oil, gas or coal. This may have happened without the impact of Just Stop Oil, but I think it is reasonable to assume that the high profile campaign may have had some positive influence. Likewise, moves to increase insulation in homes have become part of the agenda for all political parties including the government.

Ultimately the success of a movement of civil disobedience relies on numbers. If, for example, all church-goers in the UK had glued themselves to the M25, the government would probably have insulated Britain immediately! But we only have control over ourselves. And the question we must ask ourselves, instead of "do we think it's going to work?," must always be "what am I going to do to help *make* it work?"

## REVD HELEN BURNETT

*CCA member Revd Helen Burnett gave the following statement when she was in court charged with wilful obstruction of the highway.*

This is the first week of Passiontide, a time in the Christian year when the truth is revealed. This trial began with an oath on a bible—the sacred text that teaches a radical way of love and which includes the account of Jesus before Pilate when he famously replied 'what is truth' before falling silent in the face of a justice system that had nothing of real truth and justice to offer him.

Well, I'm afraid you are not going to have silence from me and I hope you can offer more than Pilate. Here is my truth, the truth of thousands of activists, and of the truth of millions too busy trying to survive, too busy grieving, too busy coping with the real live effects of the climate and ecological emergency.

On Oct 7th 2019 I was sitting on the ground, for that brief spell, a small patch of Millbank was holy ground; holy ground being held against all odds, against the state, against ecocide, against corporate power, against self—serving politics, against a fossil fuel economy and against all that contrives to damage our earth and its fragile web of life, against all that desecrates the sacred. And for a brief moment there was full autonomy, I held tight to love and to a tenacious hope. What a contrast to this space.

Mark and I stand before you, two priests, people of faith who sat in the road for their beliefs. We stand here charged and brought to court, while governments and corporations go unchallenged on countless charges of ecocide.

During the course of that day I gave an interview to the Daily Telegraph, to Christian Premier radio, spoke alongside representatives of faith based NGO's, prayed in a multi faith gathering on a bridge that was blocked by the police, helped to carry an enormous ark—a striking symbol of hope in the face of despair.

I had multiple conversations with multiple people who love and care for this planet and the people who live on it, and then I sat with people I'd never met before in solidarity with our neighbours on the other side of the globe. And I prayed, prayed in the deepest most profound way that happens, only when all else seems lost and we touch the very heart of the matter.

What kind of a mad world is it that has two vicars who can

see and understand the catastrophic harm to human, animal and plant life that is the climate catastrophe standing in a dock before you for telling the truth about an existential threat? We have looked into the abyss, seen the despair, and our hope is to find agency in whatever way we can through action and contemplation to do something before we die for a world that is dying.

As I prayed a young woman sang Bread and Roses – I want bread and roses for the world—beauty and sustenance, a sharing of life's glories, glories that should be available to all. A stranger prayed for me, and blessed me, and a police officer repeatedly said that he didn't want to arrest me, called me padre and begged me to desist because his girlfriend would never forgive him for arresting me!

Today, 17 months later it is my eldest son's 30th birthday, he is living through a pandemic that is caused by the catastrophic effects of the minority world's lifestyle. In the course of his life I have marched, signed petitions, written letters, educated myself, and many others and been a teacher, mother and priest. That vocation commits me to the fierce love and protection of my children, and of, by extension the children of the world. As a priest in the Anglican Communion my vocation brings a commitment to the 5th mark of mission, which is: 'to strive to safeguard the integrity of creation, and sustain and renew the life of the earth'.

This duty I hold in common with Christians across the globe linked by a faith that demands love for neighbour and, where necessary, demands personal sacrifice. As vicars we have the 'cure of souls'—that's not some mere ephemera that flies off to heaven—it is the fully integrated body and spirit—the spiritual and physical well-being of the people in our parishes.

With a care also for creation that then extends to the soil, the trees, and all that lies within our parish. I am called to pastoral care for people and planet in the place of my work in the parish of Chaldon where I preach that we must love our neighbour and that our neighbour is not just the person we can see, but the person we cannot see, in Bangladesh, in the Niger Delta, in the Maldives, where people are suffering as we speak from catastrophic climate change—on their behalf I claim immediate and urgent necessity.

They are my neighbour; to pass by on the other side as a member of the minority world that created the catastrophe, is not an option. My faith compels me to love my neighbour, to cross over even when it is dangerous to do so; not to turn a blind eye to the truth and pass by on the other side. By demanding action on climate change I am exercising my faith, by praying as I take action, I am exercising my right to freedom of worship in article 9 of the European Convention on Human Rights and to assemble with others in solidarity under Article 11 of the same convention.

When governments refuse to listen; when profit is the golden calf and we commodify every part of the planet; when we are crucifying our earth which will not have a risen life but which will come to an end and take with it millions of souls for whom I wish to advocate, the imperative must be to act. That imperative to love ferociously culminated for me in a moment of deep clarity and deep prayer on Monday October 7th 2019.

I knew that all that I had left at that moment between myself and the appalling climate injustice of this world, was my body to place between the oncoming disaster and the powers that be—my body, on the line, in the face of the social and economic structures that prevail, in the face of systemic refusal to face this disaster with honesty and with immediate action.

And so I prayed and my prayer was protest—that is a right enshrined in law a right to be exercised in an emergency. I did this on behalf of those who are in immediate danger and I did this for my own children and godchildren, for the children in my church and in my school, all of whom will witness in their lifetimes what happens beyond the cliff edge.

Ultimately, my faith and my understanding of the world convinces me that love must prevail. So, today when secular laws fail in their duty to protect our earth I am compelled to turn to a higher moral and spiritual authority. Perhaps this court could have the courage and the capacity to do the same....

Yes, 17 months ago I sat in the road. It was a tiny miniscule moment in the greater scheme of things and since when no change has been effected, it was my only remaining option in the face of massive negligence.

*Do not go gentle into that good night*
*Rage, rage against the dying of the light.*
Dylan Thomas

*I said to my soul, be still, and wait without hope*
*For hope would be hope for the wrong thing; wait without love,*
*For love would be love of the wrong thing; there is yet faith*
*But the faith and the love and the hope are all in the waiting.*
T.S. Eliot, *East Coker*

*Choose life*
Deuteronomy 30

*NINE*

# BEYOND HOPE

Somewhere on Crosby Beach near Liverpool in the UK can be seen 100 cast-iron, life-size figures spread out along three kilometres of the foreshore, stretching almost one kilometre out to sea. These spectacular sculptures by Antony Gormley—each one weighing 650 kilos—are made from casts of the artist's own body standing on the beach, all of them looking out to sea, staring at the horizon in silent expectation.

According to Antony Gormley, *Another Place* harnesses the ebb and flow of the tide in order to explore humanity's relationship with nature. He explains:

> The seaside is a good place to do this. Here time is tested by tide, architecture by the elements, and the prevalence of sky seems to question the earth's substance. In this work, human life is tested against planetary time. This sculpture exposes to light and time the nakedness of a particular and peculiar body. It is no hero, no ideal, just the industrially reproduced body of a middle-aged man trying to remain standing and trying to breathe, facing a horizon busy with ships, moving materials and manufactured things around the planet.[1]

The sculpture is in part, an exploration of the fragility of the human person in the face of the elements but also the vulnerability of the Earth's very substance itself.

At a different part of the UK coastline, the artist Maggi Hambling unveiled a new collaborative work, entitled *Relic*, with sound artist Chris Watson which is now permanently on display at Snape Maltings. The work is a response to the continuing melting of the polar ice caps and the artists' concern about climate change. They write: "As if on the threshold of a dream, chaos clashes with order, night meets day, primordial forms rise out of the dissolving icecap to confront the visitor with our destruction of the planet."[2]

Maggi Hambling first started making works about the melting ice sheets at the poles and confronting the issue of climate change as part of her 2017 *Edge* exhibition at the Marlborough Fine Art Gallery in London.

In St. Martin's in the Fields, in London, mud cubs: a different expression of climate awareness. *With the Heart of a Child*, seven life-size bronze children, one from every continent on Earth, hesitate in time, leaning forward, hopeful, poised to dive, eyes closed, dreaming into their future, anticipating things unseen. Their creator, Nicola Ravenscroft, writes that, "As an artist, I am visionary, sculptor, mother to many, and grandmother to even more," she breathes life into life, taking "clay, dirt and stardust, shaped and twisted torn smoothed and broken lost, found and moulded wax and singing molten bronze through white-hot crucible-refining fire, Earth's own core breathing life into revealing-truth, a giving-birth to energy."[3] The result is this installation of eco-earthling-warrior-mudcubs; children intimately connected to the earth, reminding us of our duty of care to life, to love, to planet Earth.

In a provincial town in the South West of England—an exhibition by artists seeking asylum in the UK—refugees from many parts of the world experiencing the effects of climate change much more sharply than we do in the UK—yet. In *Sound of the Earth*, a sculptor from Afghanistan speaks of the entrapment of the Earth in a technological hell—we witness a shrunken and wizened globe held caged by metal and wood. A refugee from Palestine invites the onlooker to consider how the Earth itself feels about the climate crisis, with a painting of a developer pushing the one remaining tree over the edge of a cliff into an abyss.

In the courtyard outside Somerset House in London, *Whorled*, a new commission from the Mumbai-based artist Jitish Kallat comprises two intersecting spirals, 336 metres long, that echo the signage of UK roads and connect the courtyard both to locations across the planet and the distant universe. The curator writes:

> *Whorled (Here After Here After Here)* is conceived as a seismic ripple or a galactic whorl, spiralling outwards from the centre of the courtyard. Two vast, extended scrolls form interlocking spirals and a continuum of text and symbols which follow the visual identity of the UK's road signage. These signs indicate the distance from Somerset House to locations across the planet and beyond, pointing to celestial bodies, such as the Moon, Mars, and distant stars in the Milky Way. Some of the places featured in the work have fallen victim to rising sea levels, while others are known to be under environmental threat of submersion within the next thirty years. These place names, accompanied by warning signs, resonate with Somerset House's own proximity to the River Thames and London's vulnerability to flooding. The cyclical movements through space and non-linear time prompt a reconsideration of our relationship with the planet, its past and imminent future, and the wider cosmos[4].

And in a car park in a little coastal town in the north west highlands of Scotland, a piece of raised sculpture attached to a chainmail fence, the work of 10 and 11 year olds guided by their teacher. It shows, in bright contrasting colours, the way in which the Earth's temperature has risen since 1900. A simple piece of art work, but engaging the attention and concerns of the next generation and probably replicated by other schools up and down the country.

These are six of the many manifestations of climate change awareness filtered through art and also to be found in literature, poetry, liturgy, prayer and song. Climate change has become the focus of novels and stories. Touring artworks such as *Oil Fountain*, highlighting contemporary society's reliance on oil and the huge globe, *Gaia*, both created by Luke Jerram, to be exhibited in Cathedrals, at festivals and in secular buildings, are rooted in the desire to draw attention to the fragility and wonder of planet earth as viewed from outside its boundaries, and to the danger that it is in.

Art both reveals and conceals truth and is thus an appropriate vehicle for addressing our current predicament. Climate awareness is now everywhere yet it remains nowhere. It lurks somewhere in the minds of perhaps the majority of the world's population but still mostly at a subterranean level.

*

Towards the end of 2022, I was visiting a little town in the north west highlands of Scotland and popped into the bookshop. I came across a brightly covered hardback book entitled *The Climate Book*. The coloured stripes on the cover depicted the planet's temperature rise since the beginning of the industrial revolution. The book has been created and edited by Greta Thunberg, who introduces each section with several pages of her own comment.

I bought it, and in my arrogance, I described it to the friend I was with as perhaps useful to have as a "coffee table" book about climate change. In fact, amidst the plethora of books on the market at the moment about hope, *this* is a book that offers more hope than all the rest of them. For it cuts through the "blah blah," as Greta has always described it, and offers us, not a coffee table book, but a whole library of the most up to date expertise on every conceivable aspect of the subject. It is a book to give to all one's friends wherever they are on the spectrum of knowledge and belief and commitment to the predicament we are in.

At the time of writing, Greta is still a teenager. Her part in raising awareness of the impending climate catastrophe is truly remarkable, and I want her to have the "last word" so to speak in this book. I have no idea if she is a person of faith, but she is certainly one of God's chosen instruments in waking up the world to the impending disaster with which we are faced. Thank you, Greta.

As we traverse this crucial decade, the only thing we can know for sure is that the future of the world is highly uncertain. It is also uncertain by what means we may still be able to influence that future for good. The speed and progress of climate change is undeniable. So much of the physical science is irrefutable; and yet so much of the social science, of how social systems can be changed, is still unknown. So working out ways forward for the climate movement, and for climate activism in general, is complex.

A little before COP26, an essay was published by Rupert Read in which he considers in particular the many different ways in which climate activism has manifested itself. In it he weighs up the importance of a "moderate flank," standing alongside the various radical parts of the movement—XR, Insulate Britain, Just Stop Oil, Burning Pink—finding its place and then providing a place for those many others who seek a home in which to be effective in our present predicament. He writes:

> The truly radical thing now, one might venture, is to pause, and contemplate, not just act. Accepting that we are not going to achieve a radical change overnight forces us to look into ourselves. To face the grief, terror, disappointment. To actually, honestly grasp that no-one is coming to save us; that we, en masse, are going to have to do it ourselves. The really radical thing to do is to appreciate and face honestly that it is too late for a smooth transition to a long-term viable civilisation. Once one accepts this, one's (quite understandable and correct) sense of urgency is also tempered; and then one can slow down and exit headless-chicken mode. This is one of many ways .... in which the politics our time needs is a politics of paradox.[5]

So where does hope come in? Hope is one of the three theological virtues so it cannot easily be dismissed, ignored or set aside. Yet it is difficult to engage with the concept of hope without it edging rather quickly into denial—denial of the enormity of the dire situation that we face. I appreciate, however, the words of Howard Zinn, the American historian and philosopher who wrote extensively on the civil rights and peace movements in America:

> To be hopeful in bad times is not just foolishly romantic. It is based on the fact that human history is a history not only of cruelty, but also of compassion, sacrifice, courage, kindness... What we choose to emphasise in this complex history will determine our lives. If we see only the worst, it destroys our capacity to do something. If we remember those times and places—and there are so many—where people have behaved magnificently, this gives us the energy to act and at least the possibility of sending this spinning top of a world in a different direction... And if we do act, in however small a way, we don't have to wait for some grand utopian future. The future is an infinite succession of presents and to live now as we think human beings should live, in defiance of all that is bad around us, is itself a marvellous victory.[6]

I mentioned that Josh, a young climate protester, wrote these words from prison: "For me, hope has been replaced by faith."[7] A shrewd insight; for faith gives us the purpose and stamina for action, whilst hope is the fruit of action, rather than the other way round.

But hope also emerges from a continuous exposure to, and experience of, that life force which for people of faith is perceived as the Living God. Hope finds its way into our being, despite ourselves, as we open ourselves to receive new life from the Source of life. Hope then moves us out and beyond ourselves into an active engagement with even the most seemingly hopeless situations. But faith keeps us steady, grounded, focused, because, through faith, we know ourselves to be held by the Source of life itself which is love.

Hope, as a central part of Christian belief, is not concerned with the details of worldly existence but with the future life to come; but that is not the whole story. God hopes in us, that we shall be able by God's grace, to live the eternal life that is promised us, now. *Now* is the moment that God can act in us, and only by our responding to God's action in us now can we bring about the seemingly impossible—even the work of slowing down perhaps the impending climate catastrophe itself.

St. Paul saw that if we did not have a lively hope in the resurrection to eternal life, we are of all people the most miserable, since our whole Christian life is predicated upon it. Yet the quality of that resurrected life is open to us now; it is the life force that can propel us beyond despair and discouragement (as we look around us) and on to the hope that we, even we, can be part of enabling a different ending to the story.

So there is room for hope in this life too, but only if it is based on truth. At present, the greenwashing, the lies, the distractions, the obfuscations, which are peddled by governments, the media and above all by the fossil fuel industry itself does not lead to hope of any kind.

## A LARGER PERSPECTIVE

It may be too that we can enter into a deeper understanding of the planet's destiny if we enlarge our perspective on God's creative work. On July 16th, 2022, the *Guardian* ran a leader entitled "Ravishing new images from space only deepen the cosmic mystery." It described the first images released from Nasa's James Webb telescope, giving glimpses of stars and planets being born and dying, billions of light years away.

Unlike its predecessor, the Hubble telescope, it does not circle the earth, but the sun. It marks a new milestone in the human understanding of the cosmos, but also a milestone in understanding and accepting what is not yet known or understood. The writer comments:

> We are looking at scenarios—galaxies, nebulae—that may no longer have existed millions of years before a little planet called Earth began to form... The holy grail is how the cosmos came into being, and in so doing, created life itself. Images from Saturn revealed the presence of water vapour, once more raising the possibility that life may indeed exist or have existed, elsewhere.

But until we have evidence of this, the issue remains in the realms of philosophy (and theology). The writer concludes that we are posed with a binary in which each alternative is truly mind boggling: "[E]ither life exists elsewhere, raising whole new questions as to what forms that life may take; or it doesn't, leaving the astonishing mystery of how it ever could have happened once. The only reasonable response is awe."[8]

Such musings and questions beg another one for people of faith, which is—as J.B. Phillips asked in the 1950s—whether "our God is too small."[9] If we cannot conceive of God living and moving and being present and active within the vastness of the cosmos, it is time to review our notion of God. An expanded understanding of the notion of God, and of the complexity of the cosmos, can set our concerns about what is happening to the tiny planet we call Earth in perspective. Infinite other possibilities may be being played out in other parts of the cosmos, equally as important and interesting as anything that is happening on planet Earth, even if they do not include us! A new Heaven and a new Earth has been promised and may have been created multiple times already!

Yet, it is *of course* reasonable for us to respond to these ideas by recalling, in a paraphrase of Psalm 118, that "*this* is the earth that the Lord has made; so let us rejoice and be glad in it." *This* is the home God has given to humanity to live and to enjoy, and this is the place where He calls us to act. We, humanity, have no other home but this: this precious, beautiful creation that God has made. Even if it is only the tiniest fragment of all that He has made and rejoices in, this is what He has given to *us*.

So this is our responsibility, and requires from us all that we have to give—whatever it takes, whatever the cost, whatever the future holds for it. And even if we have indeed left it all too late to prevent our ultimate social collapse, that surely does not allow us to cease our efforts and put our feet up. We would not say to a terminally ill loved one: "since you are going to die soon anyway, and I can do no more for you, I am leaving you to fend for yourself as best you can!" Scientists tell us that even preventing a fraction of a degree of warming will help to reduce the calamitous consequences of a much hotter planet. As Greta Thunberg says, "It will never be too late to save as much as we can possibly save."[10] Some of the natural world will survive the sixth extinction event, even if much of humanity does not. So the question is: do we have sufficient love and concern for the human and non-human creatures of the earth to do whatever it takes to enable at least some of them to survive?

Macy and Johnstone, in their study of *Active Hope,* write:

> We open our eyes to both the beauty of our world and the planetary emergency we're facing. When we see what we love, it reminds us of what we act for. When we recognise the danger, it gives us a strong reason to wake up, show up and play our part.[11]

We can rejoice that within the cosmos, God may well have created many other forms of life and beauty over many billions of light years, and that God's all-embracing plan includes everything that has been made, so our demise may only be the smallest event in the Divine Mind. But we also know that God has an infinite care and love for us too—even for planet Earth, this smallest of creation events. All that we have to do, to co-operate with Divine Love, is to respond in love, with infinite faith and trust and in obedience to what is required of us now.

God will remain God, whether we exist or the whole of creation exists or not. So in the end, the Christian and others of faith, do what we do for the wellbeing of life on the planet and the human race in order to give God joy—to be, as St Cecilia expressed it, "a song in the heart of God." God grieves for His beautiful creation—more than we, His creatures, ever can. So to bring God joy in this time of great darkness is a beautiful ambition—much in the way that Etty Hillsum aspired to do in the bleak horror of the extermination camp.[12]

For the future, whatever the cosmos consists of, it is God who is at its centre, not us; and its life, continuation and purpose is in God's gift, not ours. The circle of life will continue, here or in other parts of the cosmos, according to God's will and purpose, and all that we know about that will and purpose is that it is infinitely loving and caring for everything that God has made. This has to be, and can only be, our ultimate source of hope.

After the world has ended
After the silent spring
Into the waiting silence
another song begins.
Nothing is ever over,
life breathes life in its turn.
Sometimes the people listen
Sometimes the people learn.[13]

*AFTERWORD*

# WHERE ARE WE NOW?

*The climate movement has yet to find its full moral voice on the world stage but it is certainly clearing its throat - beginning to put the very real thefts and torments that ineluctably flow from the decision to mock international climate commitments alongside history's most damned crimes.*

Naomi Klein[1]

The question as to where we are now relates both to the climate crisis and to what we are doing about it. At whatever date you are reading this book, the answer to the first is that everything is likely to be much worse now than it was at the time when I was writing about it!

For example, on the day when we were slow marching in London at the end of May 2023, further extreme heat was being recorded over Asia—with all-time-high May temperatures in China, Japan, Thailand and Russia. In Canada, wildfires had forced 16,000 Canadians from their homes. The Peruvian government had proclaimed a state of emergency, deeming the arrival of the El Niño phenomenonan "imminent danger."[2]

But by the time that you, the reader, are assimilating those facts, you will no doubt have been overtaken by a whole lot more and worse information about the climate crisis; events that are taking place in your "now" but which will have been directly caused 10-30 years earlier by our and your activities. Such is the time lag between cause and effect.

Jesus tells us to read the signs of the times. He was speaking about the future sack of Jerusalem and all that that would entail, but His words are directed to all future generations including our own. If we had only "read the signs of the times" 50 years earlier and acted accordingly!

However, for the Christian, the favourable time is always *now*. God in God's great love gives us a new beginning each day, for us to live authentically within the framework of truth as we discern it. Living in community in solidarity with one another in new sustainable ways; possessing little; holding our goods in common; nurturing the land; caring for, protecting and reverencing God's beautiful creation, with its animals and insects, plants and trees—and so much more. This is a picture of how things might be and need to be in some large measure if we are to avert catastrophe; we need to be living a lifestyle so radically different from our current one that it will be barely recognisable.

So where are we now? I might use the United Nations' climate gathering—the Conference of the Parties—to explain. COP, as it is known, has been held 27 times.

Over the past near 30 years, the Conference of the Parties has tried to address the ever more obvious and urgent climate crisis by providing an international forum to review and engage with the situation as it unfolds.

After an early Earth Summit in 1992, the first Conference of the Parties took place in 1995, tasked with addressing the problem of rising global carbon and methane emissions. The theory of global warming was well established in scientific circles, but there was less visual evidence of it taking place—and what evidence there was, was hotly disputed (mostly amongst non-scientists).

The argument, then, was about its anthropogenic nature—the extent to which the changes recorded were being brought about by human activity. By the turn of the century, at least 97% of scientists were clear that the deepening climate crisis was real, and was anthropogenic in nature: requiring human intervention of the most urgent and wide-ranging kind. The scientific evidence has materialised, and UN meetings have continued—yet emissions have continued to rise steadily over the entire period.

In 2021, with COP26 taking place in Glasgow, a variety of climate protest groups from Greenpeace to Global Justice and Tearfund sought to highlight the UK Government's lack of radical action at a moment when it was in the spotlight, holding the Presidency of COP. In its 2022 World Report. Human Rights Watch stated:

> Prior to hosting the 2021 UN climate conference in October, [the UK Government] embraced ambitious emissions reduction targets—first through its national climate plan commitment to reduce emissions by 68 percent by 2030 compared to 1990 levels, and in June 2021 through a legislated target to reach a 78 percent reduction by 2035 compared to 1990 levels...... However, the UK is not on track to fulfil these commitments. Indeed, the UK continues to expand fossil fuel production and channels billions in domestic support to fossil fuels despite its commitment to phase out fossil fuel subsidies.[3]

In other words, those ambitious reduction targets, publicised immediately before COP26 to impress the gathering of the nations, were at best greenwash, and at worst, lies.

By the end of COP26, 197 countries signed up to the Glasgow Climate Pact. Countries committed themselves to accelerating their decarbonisation plans and strengthening their emissions reduction targets. Yet many of the proposals provided nothing new, and none of them laid out a rigorous, mandated plan for *binding action*. UN scientists calculated that even if all the pledges made at Glasgow were kept, they would still amount to a 2.5 degree of global warming by the end of the century. Tipping points would be breached. The earth would be too hot to sustain humanity: an uninhabitable earth.

In fact, two things needed to have happened at Glasgow. First, binding commitments regarding fossil fuels were required: urgently and immediately reducing carbon emissions, stopping all subsidies to the fossil fuel industry and leaving new fossil fuels in the ground. Second, payments to the MAPA countries (the *Most Affected Peoples and Areas*) needed to be implemented, to compensate for loss and damage incurred by the continuing use of fossil fuels in the global north and in order for them not to have to expand their use of fossil fuels themselves.

But neither happened. Shockingly, payments to these countries which were agreed in Paris in 2015 (but never paid) were deferred for *another 3 years*. The goal of a 1.5 degree rise in temperature was perhaps kept alive by a thread, and an agreement was made to come together again in Egypt in November 2022, to review how pledges were being kept and to seek a more ambitious outcome.

COP26 was seen to be the last hope of having any chance of holding the planet's temperatures well below 2 degrees and, if possible, to 1.5 degrees; it clearly failed to put in place the measures required to do so. Thus several strands of thinking developed amongst the many climate activist individuals and protest groups throughout the world after the end of the Conference.

## THE POST-GLASGOW LANDSCAPE

First, there was a continuation of nonviolent direct action and civil disobedience, focused on getting government to change policy urgently, and swiftly to cut carbon emissions. Efforts to reach out to new groups and make links with NGO's and charities were pursued, giving new possibilities and ideas for actions that might draw in, hopefully, much bigger numbers and develop much greater awareness of what has to happen to steer the world away from the brink of catastrophe. In April 2023, this culminated with The Big One, a four day gathering and protest in London focusing on the Government's lack of progress. More radical protest groups also developed - in particular Just Stop Oil.

Second, the building of a concerted effort towards establishing new consumer priorities that support life on the planet rather than destroying it: targeting corporations and companies that sell a lifestyle inimitable to sustainable living, and persuading them to change.

Third, the continuing campaign of disinvestment. Trade Unions and Churches took up this challenge and initiatives have been directed towards opening up conversations with pension funds and, in the case of the Church, with Dioceses and Synods, encouraging them to divest from all fossil fuels and commit to no re-investment.

Fourth, an effort to confront directly the fossil fuel industries, the banks that finance them and the companies that insure them, by buying shares and attending and disrupting their AGMs, by posing continuous challenges to them to end their fossil fuel activities, and switching their activities to renewables instead.

Fifth, encouraging individuals to change their lifestyle to reflect the urgent need to cut carbon emissions, by reducing or eliminating meat eating, fast fashion and travel.

Sixth, efforts to take action through legislation, showing a considerable amount of creativity in bids to effect change by legal means—see the Appendix after this chapter.

## COP27

As we approached COP27, to be held in Egypt in November 2022, more problems loomed. The fossil fuel industry began to see the developing world as an easier option for their activity. This might indeed be resisted hard by African countries, already badly affected by the activities of the fossil fuel industry; but some leaders of African countries might want to make the case for the exploitation of their own fossil fuels themselves.

Clearly, the energy needs of Africa are great, and millions live in fuel poverty and energy deprivation. Africa has massive reserves of oil and gas; but if these new fossil fuel opportunities were to be exploited, it would make the possibility of keeping anywhere near the (already largely mythical) target of 1.5 degrees impossible. Africa is rich beyond measure in sun and wind, but it requires the global north to step up to its obligations and provide the necessary infrastructure to harness these resources and make them available for the continent. That is the least we can do in order to go some way towards addressing the evils of colonialism and the legacy of empire that have caused so much destruction and harm, and to at least try to slow down runaway climate catastrophe.

COP27 was the first COP to be held on the African continent—a significant event in its own right. But would COP27 deliver anything more substantial than COP26? At the very least, it needed to rule out all new fossil fuel excavation; demand that governments impose major windfall taxes on the fossil fuel industry; and activate agreements already entered into with countries of the global south. Many were also calling for the cancellation of the debts of countries in the global south owed to the global north.

The pressures on governments to avoid, rather than address, the climate crisis, made the need for action from the grassroots more likely and more necessary. September 2022 had seen a new prime minister and a newly formed government in the UK, and few if any members of this government were viewing the climate emergency as a priority. The reversal of so many green policies meant that the project to address climate change with meaningful action seemed in tatters. The Prime Minister did, eventually, decide to attend COP27; but with so many disparate agendas at home and abroad, it was hard to see from where new initiatives for the care and succour of Mother Earth might arise.

The UN Secretary General, Antonio Guterres opened COP27 with an utterly uncompromising speech, laying out the truth of the climate crisis:

> In just days, our planet's population will cross a new threshold. The 8 billionth member of our human family will be born. This milestone puts into perspective what this climate conference is all about. How will we answer when "Baby 8 Billion" is old enough to ask: *What did you do for our world—and for our planet—when you had the chance?* Excellencies, this UN Climate Conference is a reminder that the answer is in our hands. And the clock is ticking. We are in the fight of our lives. And we are losing.[4]

His words went unheeded. If anything, COP27 was more of a disappointment than COP26. Some observers estimated that there were twice as many fossil fuel lobbyists present than in Glasgow in 2021. One of their objectives was to try and establish gas as "green" energy and to push African gas as a "transition" fuel.

The Loss and Damage agreement was achieved—where rich countries pay for the enormous infrastructure destruction inflicted on global south countries, by climate change caused by the north. This was obviously highly significant—long overdue, but much to be welcomed. In the words of the UN Secretary General, it would help to build trust between the northern and southern hemispheres. But there was no agreement about how much would be paid, who would pay for it and over what period of time.

Even more seriously, there were less robust statements about the urgent need to reduce carbon emissions now, and the equally urgent need to refrain from excavating any more new fossil fuels: coal, oil or gas. In a word, the world has kept its foot firmly on the accelerator and seems therefore to be heading towards human extinction in the not-too-distant future.

## THE BIODIVERSITY CRISIS

Alongside the climate emergency COPs are those devoted to biodiversity. The emergencies are interlinked, of course, but biodiversity loss has received far less attention. COP15, at the end of 2022, aimed at the adoption of the post-2020 global biodiversity framework: a global roadmap for the conservation, protection, restoration and sustainable management of biodiversity and ecosystems for the next decade.

One million species are at risk of extinction, with species vanishing at a rate not seen in 10 million years. The Living Planet Report 2022 is WWF's most comprehensive study to date of trends in global biodiversity and the health of our planet. The latest flagship publication reveals global wildlife populations have plummeted by 69% on average since 1970, a staggering rate of decline. The Living Planet Report tells us that between 1970 and 2018, on average, there was a 69% decline in population size across the 31,821 studied populations. Because the report is talking about averages, the rate of decline in some species is much sharper.

Negotiators hoped that the two-week UN summit would yield a deal that ensures there is more "nature"—animals, plants, and healthy ecosystems—in 2030 than that which exists now. The new goal will rely heavily on the involvement of indigenous peoples, who steward land that is home to about 80 percent of Earth's remaining biodiversity.

Some of the toughest areas to be negotiated included whether to impose a deadline for phasing out pesticides, and how to ensure poor nations will have the funding needed to restore degraded areas. On December 19th, the Conference announced an agreement for the special protection of 30% of the Earth's land surface. Something to celebrate indeed; but welcome as they are, none of the agreements have teeth—as none of them are mandatory.

# CONCLUSION

The Canadian Prime Minister Justin Trudeau commented that "if we can't agree as a world on something as fundamental as protecting nature, then nothing else matters." There is increasing awareness that protecting nature and controlling climate change go hand in hand. Healthy ecosystems such as forests, wetlands, peat bogs and seagrass beds are key to controlling global warming. At the same time, rising global temperatures are increasingly threatening many ecosystems as well as species unable to adapt quickly or to move to cooler climes.

As we learn that the next climate change COP in 2023 is to be held in Dubai City, in the petrostate of the United Arab Emirates, we might do well to recall Einstein's parable of quantum insanity: "Insanity is doing the same thing over and over and expecting the results to be different."

With this in mind, it needs to be stated unequivocably that the Conferences of the Parties have utterly failed in their task of getting their members to lower carbon emissions and have only served to lull the world into thinking that "something is being done." COPs have become servants of the fossil fuel industry and far from creating a framework for the radical economic, political and social changes that are required, have simply enabled business as usual to continue.

We have to arrive at the position—the very simple-to-state position—that we have to *just stop using all fossil fuels now*. To paraphrase Greta: we can only solve a crisis by treating it as a crisis. But self evidently this is not how we view climate change. If we did, we would say that we first have to stop using fossil fuels now and then work out how to deal with the consequences of that decision. Its not the other way round. The Government and the fossil fuel industry want us to believe that the means of exiting from fossil fuels have to be worked out first. But if we are to have an even half habitable planet, *we have to stop using fossil fuels now*. No new fossil fuels to be excavated and no existing fossil fuels in mines or depots to be accessed. We have used up all our carbon budget and reached the end of the fossil fuel road.

Since there is no likelihood that they will take and implement the draconian decisions that are required, all future COPs should be boycotted and they should be considered as targets for disruption by climate protesters.

A crisis of infinite proportions is assailing the world, requiring all that we can muster and demanding all our reserves of faith and spirituality and solidarity with one another. It demands courage, compassion, sacrifice and truth telling in great measure. We live in a climate crisis blind world, a climate crisis blind society. CCA founder member Ruth Jarman wrote to me:

> Every time we talk about the climate and biodiversity crises, we can so easily slide down the slope into "easy things we can all do," peddling the lie that "many little things all add up to big things," making us all feel comfortable by recycling and planting wild flowers, all the while carrying on eating meat, keeping the central heating on and flying off on holidays or pilgrimages.

And, I would add, failing to challenge the "powers and principalities" that are taking us over the cliff.

This is where we are now; this is the reality with which we are faced. May we somehow find the means to rise up and meet the challenge that is demanded of us. "We must become the wind and the current that diverts the oncoming storm!"[6]

# APPENDIX: LEGISLATIVE INITIATIVES

There have been plentiful efforts to take action through legislation, showing a considerable amount of creativity in their bids to effect change by legal means.*

## *Climate and Ecological Emergency Bill*

September 2020 saw the presentation to Parliament of the Climate and Ecological Emergency Bill. It brought together the two global crises of climate and biodiversity loss, underlining their interconnection.

The Bill requires the Prime Minister to achieve climate and ecology objectives; to give the Secretary of State a duty to create and implement a strategy to achieve those objectives; to establish a Citizens' Assembly to work with the Secretary of State in creating that strategy and to give duties to the Committee on Climate Change regarding the objectives and strategy.

A widespread and well organised campaign—Zero Hour—is ongoing, to get this Private Member's Bill debated, which had been presented to Parliament by Caroline Lucas, the Green MP, on September 3rd, 2020. It requires support from MPs and the Lords of all parties in order for it to be allowed to be debated in the Commons and the Lords. Then, hopefully, it can continue its passage through Parliament and become law.

If this could be achieved, it would have some hope of holding this

---

* In September 2022 more than 250 legal professionals—from junior lawyers to King's Counsel, senior partners in law firms and Professors of Law—signed an open letter drawing attention to the way in which the legal profession needs to move onto the right side of history. They called themselves 'Plan B'. This was followed some months later by 170 legal professionals making a commitment that they would not defend fossil fuel industries when they were seeking to advance their activities nor would they prosecute climate protesters. By doing so, the lawyers are in danger of breaking their juridical oath to operate a 'cab rank' system for taking on cases.

and subsequent governments to account for their action on climate change in a meaningful way.

## *Making Ecocide a Crime*

Another legislative effort to protect the environment had been floated as early as the 1970s: an attempt to make ecocide a crime.

In 2010, British barrister Polly Higgins had submitted to the United Nations an amendment to the Rome Statute, proposing that "ecocide" be legally recognised as the fifth international crime against peace.* In proposing the inclusion of ecocide, Polly Higgins was arguing for the recognition of a crime against the environment—against all of its species and creatures and against the earth itself—in order to promise and provide it with protection.

Polly died in 2019, before this great and significant effort could be brought to fruition; but in June 2021, legal experts submitted a draft law, which, if accepted by the International Criminal Court, would become the fifth International crime open to be prosecuted by law—thus offering significant environmental protection worldwide.

## *Challenging the Net Zero Strategy*

Friends of the Earth, together with the Good Law Project and Client Earth, took the government to court over its woeful Net Zero Strategy—and won, forcing it to develop a much stronger and more joined-up plan by March 2023.

The High Court found that the net zero strategy, which sets out plans to decarbonise the economy, did not meet the Government's obligations under the Climate Change Act of 2008—which required detailed climate policies that show how the UK's legally-binding carbon budgets will actually be met.

—

* At the moment, the Rome Statute acknowledges four crimes against peace: genocide; crimes against humanity; war crimes; and the crime of aggression.

It also found that parliament, and the public, were not told about a shortfall in meeting a key target to cut emissions. Friends of the Earth's experts pored over the original 400-page strategy and found it riddled with holes and omissions. For example, it was not clear whether the government had factored in the emissions that will result from its own policies, like its £27 billion road-building programme, or plans for airport expansions all over the country.

Further concerns included: there was no promise to end the use of fossil fuels; a lack of investment to fund the proposed measures; over-reliance on technology that has not been rolled out yet, such as "sustainable" aviation fuel, carbon capture and storage, and magic animal feed that stops cattle belching methane. But the major concern was that the strategy does not contain any assessment of the impact of the proposed policies – it was all theoretical. There was no way for Parliament or the public to know whether the government was going to meet its legal targets or not.

## *Other Legislative Efforts*

Friends of the Earth Cymru won a Clean Air Bill for Wales, which was included in the legislative programme for the next Senedd year. They continued to fight the government's decision to fund the vast Mozambique liquified natural gas (LNG) project with $1.5bn of taxpayer's money through its export credit agency, UK Export Finance (UKEF). The judicial review ended in legal deadlock in December 2021 when two High Court judges disagreed on the verdict and a split decision meant the case was dismissed and will have to be reconsidered. The Northern Ireland Climate Change Act got royal assent in June 2022.

## *Withdrawing from the Energy Charter Treaty*

The Energy Charter Treaty is a major obstacle to progress in eliminating fossil fuels and pursuing climate justice. It allows fossil fuel companies to sue countries for many millions of pounds if environmental protections get in the way of their profits.

So far, attempts to reform it have fallen short, and abolishing it would be costly; the UK alone could be liable for £12 billion. On the other hand, studies have shown the absurdity of staying in it, and the pressure on the UK government to withdraw from the treaty has increased. At the end of November 2022, we saw a breakthrough: the EU Commission began a coordinated EU withdrawal from the Energy Charter Treaty, which is already under way.

### *The Fossil Fuel Non-Proliferation Treaty*

Attempts are ongoing to get countries to sign up to the Fossil Fuel Non-Proliferation Treaty: designed to end all new exploration and production of fossil fuels, modelled on the Nuclear Non-Proliferation Treaty. It states that the existing production of fossil fuels has to be phased out in line with the 1.5 degrees global climate goal; and effort must be shifted towards making a just transition to renewables.

# REFERENCES


**Author's Note**

1 Dear, John, *op. cit, p.3*

**Introduction**

1 Gupta Saloni, Rouse Barry T., Sarangi Pranita P., "Did Climate Change Influence the Emergence, Transmission, and Expression of the COVID-19 Pandemic?" *Front Med* (Lausanne), Vol. 8 (December 2021).
2 Beyer, Robert M. et al., "Shifts in global bat diversity suggest a possible role of climate change in the emergence of SARS-CoV-1 and SARS-CoV-2," *Science in the Total Environment*, Vol. 767 (May 2021).
3 Symposium of Episcopal Conference of Africa and Madagascar (SECAM) Press Conference: *African Climate Dialogues Communiqué* (October 17 2022).

**A Crisis Like No Other**

1 Robinson, Elmer and Robbins, Robert C., "Sources, Abundance and Fate of Gaseous Atmospheric Pollutants," unpublished report prepared for American Petroleum Institute (1968).
2 McGuire, Bill, *Hothouse Earth* (London: Icon Books, 2022), pp. 22-23.
3 Verbruggen, Aviel, "The Geopolitics of Trillion US$ Oil & Gas Rents," *International Journal of Sustainable Energy Planning and Management*, Vol. 36 (2022), pp. 3-10.
4 Carson, Rachel, *Silent Spring* (New York: Houghton Miffin, 1962).
5 Freeman, Martha, ed., *Always Rachel: The Letters of Rachel Carson and Dorothy Freeman 1952-1964 (Concord Library)* (Boston: Beacon Press, 1994).
6 Wheeler Wilcox, Ella, "Protest," in *Poems of Problems* (Chicago, W.B. Conkey Co.,1914).
7 Dixon Philip, "Lament for Six Giraffes," (unpublished poem 2022).
8 Westveer, J, et. Al., *A Deep Dive into the Living Planet Index: A Technical Report* (Gland, Switzerland: World Wildlife Fund, 2022), p.4
Bar-on, Yinon M., Phillips, Rob, Milo, Ron, "The biomass distribution on Earth," *PNAS*, Vol. 115, no. 25 (May 2018).

9 Wallace-Wells, David, *The Uninhabitable Earth: Life after Warming*. (New York: Tim Duggan Books, 2019), p.188.

10 Foote, Eunice, "Circumstances Affecting the Heat of the Sun's Rays," *American Journal of Scientific Arts*, Vol. 22, no. 66 (1856) 382–383.

11 McGuire, op. cit., p. 19

12 McKie, Robin, "Cop27 climate summit: window for avoiding catastrophe is closing fast," *The Guardian* (30 October 2022).
Lenton, Timothy M., Rockström, Johan et al., "Climate Tipping Points — too risky to bet against: The Growing Threat of Abrupt and Irreversible Climate Changes must Compel Political and Economic Action on Emissions," *Nature*, Vol. 575, no. 7784 (November 2019), pp. 592-595.

13 Pörtner, H.O. et al., ed.. *Climate Change 2022: Impacts, Adaptation, and Vulnerability*. Contribution of Working Group II to the Sixth Assessment Report of the Intergovernmental Panel on Climate Change (Cambridge: Cambridge University Press, August 2022).

14 Lynn, Matthew, "The UN's 'scientific' climate report is nothing more than confected hysteria," *Daily Telegraph* (20 March, 2023).

15 Carrington, Damian, "World on brink of five 'disastrous' climate tipping points, study finds," *The Guardian* (8 September 2022).
McKay, David I. Armstrong ; Rockström, Johan et al., "Exceeding 1.5 °C global warming could trigger multiple climate tipping points," *Science*, Vol. 377, no. 6611 (2022).

16 Hook, Leslie and Campbell, Chris, "Methane hunters: what explains the surge in the potent greenhouse gas?" *Financial Times* (23 August 2022).
United Nations Environment Programme (UNEP), *Global Methane Assessment 2030: Baseline Report* (2022).

17 Kemp, Luke et al., "Climate Endgame: Exploring catastrophic climate change scenarios", *PNAS*, Vol. 119, no. 34 (August 2022).

18 Grey, Carmody, Lecture given at St. George's Church, London (2021).

19 Klein, Naomi, *Hot Money* (UK, Penguin Books, 2014, pages 26-27); see also *This Changes Everything* (New York, Simon Schuster, 2014).

20 Klein, Ibid. p. 77.

21 Schreiber, Melody, "Addressing Climate Change Concerns in Practice," *American Psychology Association*, Vol. 52, no. 2 (March 2021).

22 Hickman, C., Marks, E., et al. "Climate Anxiety in Children and Young People and their beliefs about Government Responses to Climate Change: a Global Survey," *Lancet Planetary Health*, Vol 5, no.12, December 2021).

23 Royal College of Psychiatrists, *Position Statement PS03/21: Our Planet's Climate and Ecological Emergency* (May 2021), p. 17.

24 McMichael, A.J. et al., "Global environmental change and health: Impacts, Inequalities, and the Health Sector," *BMJ*, Vol. 336, no.191 (2008).
25 Rao, Mala and Powell Richard A., "An Overview of the Mental Health Impacts of the Climate Crisis - The Climate Crisis and the Rise of Eco-Anxiety," *The BMJ Opinion* (October 2021).
26 Ibid.
27 Randall, Rosemary, and Hoggett, Paul, "Engaging with Climate Change: Comparing the Cultures of Science and Activism," *Environmental Values*, Vol. 27, no. 3 (2018), pp. 223-243.
28 Cohen, Zoe, Whybrow, Alison & Aspey, Linda, "Call for Multi-pronged Coaching Response to the Global Climate Crisis," *Coaching at Work*, Vol. 4, no. 5 (October 2019).
29 Walrond-Skinner, Sue, *Family Therapy - The Treatment of Natural Systems* (London, Routledge, 1976).
30 Kearney, Phil, "The systemic crisis of climate change: clinical and political reflections," *Feedback: Journal of the Family Therapy Association of Ireland* (2013), pp. 42-50.
31 Randall and Hoggett, op. cit.
32 Pope Francis, *Laudato Si'* (Rome: Papal Encyclical, 2015).
33 Schumacher, E.F., *Small is Beautiful* (London: Blond and Briggs, 1973), p.5.
34 Lovelock, James, *Gaia: A New Look at Life on Earth* (Oxford: OUP, 1979).
35 *IEA, World Energy Outlook 2021*, (IEA: Paris, 2021).
Quiggin, Daniel et al, *Climate Change Risk Assessment 2021* (London: Chatham House, 2021).
36 Kearney, op. cit., 45-46.

**Faith, Spirituality and Solidarity**

1 Wright, Stephen and Jenkins, Cat, "Faith in a Time of Collapse," *Church Times* (4 November 2022)
2 Bendell, Jem, "Deep Adaptation: A Map for Navigating Climate Tragedy," Unpublished IFLAS Occasional Paper 2, Revised 2nd Edition (27July 2020).
3 Macy, Joanna and Johnstone, Chris, *Active Hope* (California, New World Library, 2022), p.9
4 Bateson, Gregory, *Steps to an Ecology of Mind: Collected Essays in Anthropology, Psychiatry, Evolution and Epistemology* (New York, Ballantine Books, 1972)
5 Macy and Johnstone, *op. cit*, p.228

6 Thunberg, Greta, "It's never too late to do as much as we can," Interview with Andrew Marr, BBC News (29 October 2021).
7 McKibben, Bill, *The End of Nature* (New York, Random House, 1989); *Eaarth: Making a Life on a Tough New Planet* (New York, Henry Holt and Co., 2010); *An Idea Can Go Extinct* (New York, Penguin Books, 2021)
8 Vince, Gaia, *Nomad century: How to Survive the Climate Upheaval* (London, Allen Lane, 2022)
9 Harmon, Caroline, "The Story of Christian Climate Action" in *Time to Act*, ed. Williams, Jeremy (London, S.P.C.K., 2020).
10 Williams, Rowan, Endorsement of *Time to Act, CCA resource book*, ed. Williams, Jeremy (London: SPCK, 2020).
11 Randall, R. and Hoggett, P., *op. cit*
12 Smith, Josh, *Prison Diary* (Unpublished, 2021)
13 Nikki Jones, Energy News, Bristol
14 See https://www.deepadaptation.info
15 Jackson, Catherine, "In focus: facing the reality of climate change," *Therapy Today* Vol 31, no. 2 (March 2020).

**Following Jesus**

1 Dear, John, *The Sacrament of Civil Disobedience* (1994; 2nd edition, Coventry: Lab/Ora Press 2022), p.30
2 Pagola, Jose Antonio, *Jesus: An Historical Approximation* (Miami: Convivium Press, 2013).
3 Jenkins, David, *The Rebel Jesus*, unpublished monograph (2022), p. 21.
4 Myers, Ched, *Binding the Strong Man - A Political Reading of Mark's Gospel* (Maryknoll, New York: Orbis Books,1988), pp 81-82.
5 Ibid., p. 161.
6. Wink, Walter, *Jesus and Nonviolence - A Third Way* (Minneapolis: Augsberg Fortress, 2003).
7 Dear, op. cit., p 52.

**Why We Break the Law**

1 Sharp, Gene, *The Politics of Nonviolent Action*, 3 vols (Boston: Porter Sargent, 1973).
2 Chenoweth, Erica, *Civil Resistance - what Everyone Needs to Know* (New York, Oxford University Press, 2021).
3 King, Martin Luther, *Letter from a Birmingham Jail* (American Friends Service Committee, 1963).
4 Thoreau, Henry David, "On the Duty of Civil Disobedience" in *Walden*

*and Civil Disobedience* (New York: New American Library, 1960 [1849]).
5 Grey, Carmody, "Conversation in a Laudato Si' group on about finding courage" Facebook group. (April 14th 2023).
6 Villa-Vicencio, Charles, *Between Christ and Caesar: Classic and Contemporary Texts on Church and State*, (Grand Rapids, Michigan: William B. Eerdmans, 1986), pp. 89-99.
7 King, Martin Luther, op. cit.
8 Berrigan, Daniel, 1993, *Whereon to Stand: The Acts of the Apostles and Ourselves* (Baltimore: Fortkamp Pub. Co.,1993).
9 Gros, Frédéric, *Disobey!*, (London: Verso, 2021), p. 7.
10 Dear, op.cit., p. 168.
11 Dear, op. cit., p.4.
12 Chenoweth, Erica, op. cit., pp. 61-62.
13 Nichols, Joel A. and McCarty, James W., "When the State is Evil: Biblical Civil (Dis)Obedience in South Africa," *St. John's Law Review*, Vol. 85, no.2 (Spring 2011), Article 9.

**Prayer, Discernment and Training**

1 Jo Rand, Mark Coleman and Hilary Bond, "Arrestable? Three Stories to help you decide", in Williams, Jeremy, ed., *op. cit*, p.215
2 *ibid.*
3 Lindo, Samantha, "In Court - Right where I am supposed to be," in Williams, Jeremy, ed., *ibid* p.150
4 Newell, Martin, "Reflecting on Time Spent in Prison," talk given to CCA (27 August 2021)
5 Trowland, Morgan, Web blog post (May 2023)
6 Dear, John, *op. cit*, p.184
7 Kittle, Simon, "The Ethics of Civil Disobedience" (in Williams, Jeremy, ed., *op. cit*, p.29)
8 Lawson, Andrea, *The Entangled Activist - Learning to Recognise the Master's Tools* (London, Perspectiva Press, 2022)

**Speaking Truth**

1 Dear, op. cit., p. 243.
2 Gandhi, Mahatma, "Statement in the Great Trial of 1922," in *The Selected Works of Mahatma Gandhi*, Vol. 5, *The Voice of Truth*, ed. Shriman Naryan (Ahemedabad: Navajivan Publishing House, 1968), 40-54 (46).
3 Parfitt, Sue, Insulate Britain Press Release (12 January 2023).

4 Nixon, David, Insulate Britain Press Release (7 February 2023).
5 Pritchard, Amy, Insulate Britain Press Release (2 March 2023).
6 Mansfield, Michael, written testimony, "Top UK Lawyers Attend Insulate Britain Contempt Hearing," YouTube (3 March 2023).
7 Dear, op. cit., p. 238.
8 Ibid., 244.
9 Godlee, Fiona, "Breaking: Court finds Doctors for XR not guilty for Lambeth Bridge blockade," XR Press Release (15 November 2022).
10 Hart, Patrick, ibid.
11 Pliny, "Letter to Trajan," *Letters of Pliny* no. 96, trans William Melmoth, ed. F.T. Bosanquet, Project Gutenberg (2001).
12 Eusebius, *The History of the Church from Christ to Constantine*, trans. Williamson, G.A. (New York: Dorset Press, 1984).
13 Louth, Andrew (ed.) *Early Christian Writings*, trans Staniforth, Maxwell (London: Penguin Books, 1987).
14 Frend, W.H.C.,*The Rise of Christianity* (Philadelphia, Fortress Press: 1984), p. 319.
15 Heffernan, Thomas J., *The Passion of Perpetua and Felicity* (Oxford: Oxford University Press, 2012). Musurillo, Herbert, ed. and trans.,"The Passion of Saints Perpetua and Felicity," in The Acts of the Christian Martyrs (Oxford: Oxford University Press, 1972).
16 Mandela, Nelson, *Long Walk to Freedom* (London: Little, Brown and Co., 1994), p. 422.

**The Cost**

1 Newell, Martin, talk given to Christian Climate Action (21 August 2021).
2 Sharp, op. cit.
3 Newell, 27 August 2021 op. cit.
4 Newell, 27 August 2021 op. cit.
5 Thoreau, op. cit.
6 Dear, op. cit., p. 254.
7 Mandela, op. cit.
8 Berrigan, Daniel, *Lights on in the House of the Dead* (New York: Doubleday and Co., 1974), p.131.
9 Berrigan, ibid.
10 Berrigan, Daniel, ibid. and *Widen the Prison Gates* (New York: Touchstone Books, 1973); "Imprisonment could hardly be more to the point," *National Catholic Reporter* (11 February 1994).
11 Berrigan, see above.

12 Dear, op. cit.
13 Bonhoeffer, *Letters and Papers from Prison* (New York: Simon & Schuster, 1951) and *The Cost of Discipleship* (New York: Simon & Schuster, 1951).
14 Hillesum Etty, *An Interrupted Life. The Diaries and Letters of Etty Hillesum 1941-1943* (London: Persephone Books, 1999).
15 Trowland, Morgan, "A Message from prison – Just Stop Oil Protester Morgan Trowland," Web Blog Post, Chamberlin, Shaun, darkoptimism.org (7 May 2023)

**Do You Think It's Going to Work?**

1 Gros, op. cit., p.7.
2 Klein, op. cit., p.18.
3 Weintrobe, Sally, *Psychological Roots of the Climate Crisis: Neoliberal Exceptionalism and the Culture of Uncare* (London: Bloomsbury Academic, 2021).
4 Climate Change Committee, Progress Report to Parliament (June 2022), p. 64
5 Lawson, Alex, "Closure of coal power station set to be delayed to prevent UK blackouts," *The Guardian* (28 August 2022).
6 Williams, Rowan et al. Letter in *The Guardian*, (26 October 2018).
7 Sharp, op. cit., p. 57.
8 Gros, op. cit., p. 145.
9 "New ONS figures reveal cold homes death toll," National Energy Action (27 November 2020).
10 Highways England, "£27billion roads investment to support 64,000 jobs," Gov.UK press release (21 August 2020).
11 Williams, Rowan, Interview at Interfaith gathering in London November 2022, qtd in Cumiskey, Lucas, "Ex-Archbishop of Canterbury urges government to do more to combat climate change," *The Independent* (13 November 2022).
12 "UN Human Rights chief urges UK to reverse 'deeply troubling' Public Order Bill," UNHR press release (27 April 2023).
13 Carrington, Damian, "Huge UK public support for direct action to protect environment – poll," *The Guardian* (24 October 2022).
14 Smith, Matthew, "Concern for the environment at record highs," YouGov.uk press release (5 June 2019).
15 Davis, Colin, "Just Stop Oil: do radical protests turn the public away from a cause? Here's the evidence," *The Conversation* (21 October 2022).

**Beyond Hope**

1 Gormley, Antony, qtd in "Another Place," Regenerus.
2 Watson, Chris, "Relic: Maggi Hambling and Chris Watson," Web blog post (May 21 2021).
3 Ravenscroft, Nicola, qtd in "'With the heart of a Child': a sculpture installation and exhibition by Nicola Ravenscroft," St Martin-in-the-Fields.
4 "Whorled [Here After Here After Here]," Somerset House.
5 Read, Rupert, "What next on climate? The need for a new moderate flank," *Perspectiva* (6 October 2021).
6 Zinn, Howard, *You can't be neutral on a moving train* (Boston: Beacon Press, 2002), p. 208.
7 Smith, Josh, op. cit.
8 Guardian editorial, "The Guardian view on the James Webb telescope: a window on the unknown," *The Guardian* (16 July 2022).
9 Phillips, J.B., *Your God is too Small* (London, Epworth Press 1952). Duncan Forbes in his book *An Ecology of the Heart - Faith through the Climate Crisis* (Oxford, SLG Press, 2023), approaches some of the issues raised in this chapter in a similar way.
10 Thunberg interview, op. cit.
11 Macy and Johnstone op. cit., p. 238.
12 Hillsum, op. cit.
13 Gaiman, Neil, "After Silence for Rachel Carson," In *A Paradise of Poems*, podcast by Camellia Yang (21 July 2021).

**Afterword: Where Are We Now?**

1 Klein op. cit., p. 402.
2 "Christians arrested urging government to just stop oil," Christian Climate Action (31 May 2023)
3 Human Rights Watch, "United Kingdom, Events of 2021," *World Report* (2022).
4 Guterres, António, "Secretary-General's remarks to High-Level opening of COP27 - as delivered," United Nations (7 November 2022).
5 "Global Land Outlook 2," United Nations Convention to Combat Desertification (2022).
6 Narokobi, Bernard, "Pacific Identity and Solidarity," p. 29, qtd by Enns, Elaine and Myers, Ched, *Healing Haunted Histories: a Settler Discipleship of Decolonization* (Eugene (OR): Cascade Books, 2021), p. 273.

# ABOUT SUE PARFITT

Sue Parfitt is a member of Christian Climate Action. She practised as a family therapist throughout her working life and has written several books on family therapy under her birth name, Walrond-Skinner. She was ordained a priest in 1994 when the Church of England first admitted women to the priesthood. After retiring she has worked alongside destitute asylum seekers and spent time in Palestine, helping out with various projects but now spends most of her time committed to the climate crisis, in solidarity with others in a new community of resistance and grace.

www.labora.press

9 781739 716288

Printed by BoD™in Norderstedt, Germany